CW01369378

Virginia Woolf's
ENGLISH HOURS

PETER TOLHURST

FOREWORD
RONALD BLYTHE

BLACK DOG
BOOKS

First published in England 2015, Black Dog Books,
104 Trinity Street, Norwich, Norfolk, NR2 2BJ,
www.blackdogbooks.co.uk

Text © Peter Tolhurst, Foreword © Ronald Blythe

All rights reserved. No part of this publication may be reproduced, stored in a retrieval system, or transmitted in any form or by any means, electronic, mechanical, photocopying, recording or otherwise, without the prior permission of the copyright holders.

A CIP record of this book is available from the British Library.

ISBN 978-0-9565672-5-3

Printed in Great Britain by Berforts, Eynsham, Oxford

Picture Credits

Dust jacket, Science Museum; Frontispiece, 44, 64a, 71a, 101a, National Portrait Gallery; 1, 5a, 7, 120a, 141, 155, 156, Harvard Theatre Collection, the Houghton Library; 2, 3b, 4, 5b, 6, 12, 15, 17, 19, St Ives Museum; 3a, South Devon Railway Trust; 8, 98, 136, 165, Henrietta Garnett; 14, Tate St Ives/Private collection; 24, the estate of Dame Laura Knight; 25, 27 Bebhinn Par for Corby Castle; 54, Fitzwilliam Museum; 56a & b, Wilton House; 59, Edwin Smith/RIBA; 62b, Jonathan Gaunt; 63, 121a, 125, Dorset County Museum; 68, 69b, Giggleswick School; 81a Arthur Rivett; 88, David Fox; 99, Rye Castle Museum; 101b, Houghton Library, Harvard University; 103, 151, 158, 159, Anne Ullman; 118, Rochdale City Art Gallery; 119, Tate Archive; 122, Tim Hawkins; 129, West Sussex Record Office; 130a, Vanessa Curtis; 130b, 138, 152, 153, East Sussex Record Office; 148, 149, National Trust; 158, Graves Art Gallery, Sheffield; 162, Christopher Dalton

Acknowledgements

I must firstly place on record my thanks to the Random House Group for permission to quote from the works of Virginia Woolf. I am in addition most grateful to all those who, over the years, have so generously supplied images and information or who have welcomed me into their homes. My thanks in particular to Bebhinn Par for Corby Castle; Philip Bye, Senior Archivist, East Sussex CC; Mr and Mrs Charles Morris, Blo' Norton Hall; Sue Allen, Poniou, nr Zennor; Sue Bedford, Talland House, St Ives; Alyson Cheng, The Moat House, Warboys; Barbara Grant, Archivist, Giggleswick School; Giles Bowring, Lawkland Hall and Helen Gibson, Dorset County Museum. My thanks also to Sheila Wilkinson of the Virginia Woolf Society who kindly read through the draft ms, made a number of valuable suggestions and drew my attention to a number of inaccuracies. Any that remain are entirely my own.

Peter Tolhurst

CONTENTS

	Foreword	*i*
	Introduction	*v*
I	CORNWALL	1
II	THE BORDERS	25
III	THE FENS	32
IV	THE NEW FOREST	44
V	WILTSHIRE	51
VI	THE YORKSHIRE DALES	67
VII	EAST ANGLIA	79
VIII	RYE and ROMNEY MARSH	97
IX	SOMERSET	107
X	DORSET	117
XI	SUSSEX	128
	Bibliography	167
	Notes	169
	Index	174

For Jan

Foreword

This is a delightful account of Virginia Woolf's experience of England as against, for example, that of Henry James' and is interwoven with Peter Tolhurst's travels to what she saw from Cornwall to the Roman Wall. How do her descriptions bear up all these years later? Sometimes wonderfully well, sometimes hauntingly, always excitingly. She leaves a mark in her wake and he sees it. When Henry James declared that 'Summer afternoon – summer afternoon; to me those have always been the two most beautiful words in the English language' he would have been thinking of a Victorian countryside. Virginia Woolf insisted more than once that she was an Edwardian, by which she meant a free woman who could move about beyond the old conventions. She praised fine weather but would walk or cycle in wind and rain. This physical zest contrasted with her emotional fragility. Her domestic arrangements alone should, one would have thought, have slowed her down as a traveller-writer, for 'place' was a key element in her novels, yet she never lacked both time and strength to wander about, to look, to feel and to record. There were forays with Leonard to Scotland and the Continent, sometimes in the Singer motorcar, but *English Hours* concentrates her journeys on 'home'. This was the period when the English abroad felt obliged to write long descriptions of scenery and of food, manners, etc. They fill Virginia's letters from Brittany and Italy. But Norfolk or especially Cornwall brought a very different response, and it is this which Peter Tolhurst has gone in search of, and which has created this remarkable book.

Virginia Woolf's life was gregarious but at the same time solitary, even lonely. It is not an unusual thing for many writers – to be in a group and yet out of it. Those closest to her, her husband Leonard and her sister Vanessa, seemed to comprehend this, for they allowed their protection of her to stay hidden. They were frequently with her on these English outings and holidays but her accounts of them, although full of Bloomsbury Groupism, are dominated by that distinctive voice. It speaks to us wherever she happens to be and Peter Tolhurst catches its undertones. Some of her ventures are not especially beautiful or even interesting but these defects themselves bring something compelling to them. What she saw, heard, felt, would be hoarded away until a belated appearance in a story or maybe in one of those lengthy review-essays in the *Guardian* or *The Times Literary Supplement*. Or in gossip. These annual breaks with discipline would encourage often wild interpretations of villages and small towns, hotels and ramshackle country houses, not to mention the locals, or reveal her considerable natural history, and now and then flaunt her agnosticism. She could be quite a dangerous visitor. Her strong unguarded opinions are undiminished by the years. She writes as though she had never read a guidebook and as if a view could be marred if she did. Creature comforts or entertainment were low on the list, as was fine weather, atmosphere – although she did not call it this – very high.

Talland House in St Ives would seem to have set the pattern but whilst her girlhood holidays in Cornwall were many weeks long, those in the Fens, Rye, Somerset and Dorset were comparatively brief and often hugely athletic and resolute rather than recreational. She would see what most people missed and hear old noises. She was wary of becoming some reliable witness of where she happened to be. Writing to her sister, she asked, 'Do you like descriptions of nature? Or do you skip?' Correspondence then could be embedded in well-informed accounts of a region's stones and plants, climate or geography generally. But when Virginia mentions such things, it is with her own vision of them and on her own terms. Walking or driving to where they still are, Peter Tolhurst recognises what drew her attention, sometimes nearly a century ago, and then says what is there now or what she felt at Max Gate, Thomas Hardy's house, for instance. Here her pen was uncontrollably sharpened for 'greatness', as it so often was. But as for most of us, a place could be suffused in the work of a regional genius, artist or poet, and she was never above reverence. At the opposite end she could be thrilled by sheer lumpenness, a dull track, a view with nothing in it, a leaden stream, a bird in the wind.

Although these travels could be far from home, Virginia's life there was extraordinarily peripatetic for a woman of her time – and for her state of mind. She commuted from Tavistock Square, Richmond and Sussex most weeks, and both in country and town she was hostess to endless visitors, and guests to many friends. But at Monks House there was always a stillness in which to write. It waited for her wherever she happened to be. Her holidays provided her homecomings, and these were hugely important. To return to routine. To listen to the servants singing, to tie-up Hogarth Press books in brown paper parcels, to scratch away at a new chapter, to drive over to Charleston or to Knole. Or just to walk in London.

FOREWORD

'... you choose to sit in the mud in Kent.... [whilst] almost every day I take my walk through the City. I like it better than Kent – Bread Street, Camomile Street, Seething Lane, All Hallows, St Olaves – Then out one comes at the Tower, and there I walk on the terrace by the guns, with the ships coming up and down ...'

She is mocking the country-house view of life to her friend Vita Sackville-West. This 1930s London, especially by the Thames, would have been pretty filthy and she was writing in November. But one gets the gist. For her London could never be written off. She was no escapee and neither was her circle. But it made the rest of England strangely interesting. Especially when one was so deliberately uninformed about it. She could confront architecture with a clean slate, but many other things with an acute knowledge, and climate with a kind of genius, so that it is impossible to be in her old brief lodgings without a touch of her sun or rain. And here one must mention the photographs. They are a treasure in themselves. One finds oneself poring over them, 'seeing' that slight figure in the window, on the hotel steps, signing the register, pushing her bike. When Virginia Woolf explores a place she does not find what we know is there, but something 'other'. But what is she looking for? *English Hours* could tell you.

Today's common reader and walker, following these routes, will be in both the recent past and the present, and at the same time in fresh territory. Often freed for a few days from the strictly self-imposed pattern of toil Virginia can be like a girl out of school, exultant, carefree.

This is how Peter Tolhurst follows her to Blo' Norton Hall near Diss. It is 1906 and a cousin of Henry James has sub-let it to the Stephen sisters for the whole of August. The double visit, Tolhurst's and their's, is typical of the beautiful welding of their separate glimpses of the isolated house. This marriage of impressions governs *English Hours* throughout.

'On arrival along dusty lanes from Diss Station, Virginia immediately felt herself soothed by a wonderful tranquillity.

"... every mile seems to draw a thicker curtain than the last between you & the world. So that finally, when you are set down at the Hall, no sound what ever reaches your ear; the very light seems to filter through deep layers; & the air circulates slowly, as though it had but to make the circuit of the Hall, & its duties were complete."

'... The following day the two sisters set out to explore "a strange, lonely kind of country", an enchanted land that at first seemed both soporific and deserted:

"The corn brims the fields; but no one is there to cut it; the churches hold up broad gray fingers all over the landscape, but no one, save perhaps the dead at their feet, attend to their commands; the windmills sail round & round, but no one trims their sails; it is very characteristic that the only sign of life in the land should be that produced by the wind of Heaven." Blo' Norton Hall has a pair of brick gables that were 'coloured like an apricot in the sun'.

Who would not read on? Who would not themselves travel this way, Virginia Woolf's *Diaries* and *Letters* in hand and not always a Pevsner, plus Peter Tolhurst's interpretation of them, to discover again the England of her day? Frequently unwell, always working, reporting what she did and where she was to friends, these short tours of hers are a revelation of the old countryside. He calls it 'her own prescriptive formula of walking plus writing' and that it 'served her well through much of her time in Sussex' but that it was 'a fragile construct and one easily dislodged, especially when its very foundation was threatened.' By which he means the Battle of Britain planes above Rodmell, the destruction of Tavistock Square and for her an imminent German invasion, her husband's Jewishness, and a repetition of the wartime horrors she had gone through only twenty years earlier. He brings her to that fatal walk to the river with great understanding and tenderness.

Virginia Woolf wrote from a quiet centre which was diamond-hard and these holidays and excursions should have shown her being let off the leash. Or simply resting. Or being refreshed But she was not capable of any of these things. She was either wound up into a constant brilliance or wound down into darkness. But through these extremes the English landscape spoke to her in its individual way, as it does to each one of us, and it is this personal voice which Peter Tolhurst catches. He also recognises how the same pen which created *Night and Day, The Years,* and *Mrs Dalloway* was at work wherever she went. Wit, lyricism and marvellous descriptive powers were at work throughout her travels. She observed the rites of her class and age, the going-out in all weathers, the somehow not wanting to have over-many facts to dull first impressions, and to put on a page what she saw.

The reader never quite sees what he expects to see, but something other. And this is due to Virginia's powerful luminosity, her lighting up of ordinary things. Peter Tolhurst, like the ceaselessly discovering writer he is, has gone to see with his own eyes the places she witnessed whilst at the same time relishing everything she thought of them. What she would have made of his pilgrimage one dare not think, but we are glad that he went where she did, sometimes a century or more ago.

Ronald Blythe

Introduction

Throughout her life Virginia Woolf was engaged in a passionate affair with the English countryside. Few writers, according to Jan Morris, 'have ever been more powerfully inspired by the sense of place'[1] and Virginia's often exhilarating response to landscape, set down in letters, essays and in her diaries, nurtured her genius as a writer and provides the reader with a fascinating insight into the creative process. In 'Portraits of Places' (1906) a young Virginia Stephen reveals a love of maps and suggests their study as the best way to become acquainted with a stretch of countryside:

> For some reason there is more of the character of a place in this sheet of coloured paper, with its hills of shaded chocolate, its seas of spotless blue, and its villages of dots and punctures than in all the words of an ordinary vocabulary, arrange them how you will. The swarm of names, the jagged edge of the coastline, the curves that ships make ploughing round the world, are all romantic grains of fact brewed from the heart of the land itself …[2]

This early piece of journalism was prompted by the selection of Henry James travel essays which had appeared in this country as *English Hours* a year earlier. James had been a friend of Leslie Stephen, a regular visitor to Talland House and a shadowy presence throughout Virginia's childhood, remaining 'a portentous figure looming large and undefined in the consciousness of writers'[3] until his death in 1916. Virginia reviewed more of his work than of any living author and while she found him at times daunting, declared him a great writer.

Leslie Stephen had been an advocate of the great outdoors and it was while accompanying him on long hikes across the Cornish peninsula that his younger daughter first acquired a taste for the open road. But following the death of his wife Julia in 1895, Virginia's father never again set foot in this remote corner of England. It became a forbidden land until, with his own demise, Virginia felt able to return for the first time in a decade and she was soon out on the hills above St Ives retracing her steps 'so that the map of the land becomes solid in my brain'.[4] A year later she was in Norfolk writing to Violet Dickinson in buoyant mood:

Nessa paints windmills in the afternoon, and I tramp the country for miles with a map, leap ditches, scale walls and desecrate churches, making out beautiful brilliant stories every step of the way ...[5]

This was Virginia's way of reading a landscape shaped at every step by layers of human activity. '[T]he country is a very solid and ancient place'[6] she decided, 'there is scarcely a field in England that is not, as Mr Henry James has it, "richly suggestive".'[7] Indeed the scenic possibilities of scale and vista, of atmosphere and the historic sense, have been so celebrated that we seem to appreciate landscape through the eyes of those who have gone before and seen more clearly. Referring to the Lake District Virginia asked 'Shall we ever ... see these famous hills with our own eyes as though Wordsworth had never lived?'[8]

In 1917 while reviewing Edward Thomas' book on the subject she was already aware of what motivates the literary pilgrim. In searching for what Thomas refers to as the 'sense of England' she acknowledges 'we turn ... to Borrow, Hardy, the Brontës, Gilbert White'.[9] This is precisely what she had done in November 1904 on a trip to the nation's most potent literary shrine. On arrival in Haworth armed with a copy of Mrs Gaskell's *Life of Charlotte Brontë* she posed the question 'I do not know whether pilgrimages to the shrines of famous men ought not to be condemned as sentimental journeys ...'.[10] Her interest in the Brontë parsonage, a house 'tenanted by genius,' was partly professional – Haworth became the subject of an early essay – and she felt the trip worthwhile by her own standards. 'Curiosity is only legitimate when the house of a great writer or the country in which it is set adds something to our understanding of his books.'[11]

Virginia returned to this theme the following year when reviewing 'two trashy books'[11A] in the Pilgrimage Series. Even though the writers concerned – Thackeray and Dickens – were decidedly metropolitan she felt that each 'may be said to possess a spiritual sovereignty which no one else can dispute'.[12] In her 1932 article 'Great Men's Houses' she declares 'It is no frivolous curiosity that sends us to ... Carlyle's house and Keats' house. We know them from their houses'.[13] From the tables where they worked, the gardens they walked in and the books they read writers are brought alive again and although she had once concluded that 'a writer's country is a territory within his own brain'[14] she continued to be fascinated by the relationship between landscape and literature.

INTRODUCTION

Soon after her marriage in 1912 she travelled to Somerset with Leonard, a copy of *Lyrical Ballads* and Dorothy Wordsworth's *Journal* intent on retracing the steps of the Romantic Poets only to find the Quantocks shrouded in mist. The holiday in Dorset with Maynard Keynes in 1923 proved more successful. From Studland Bay the Woolfs were taken on a tour of places immortalised in Hardy's fiction, a prelude to Virginia's own literary pilgrimage three years later to Max Gate for tea with the great Dorset novelist.

Virginia's own sense of place took root as a child in Cornwall. Once her father had discovered Talland House with its sweep of the bay and Godrevy lighthouse it became the base for family holidays throughout her childhood. Images from those long, idyllic summers, 'the best beginning to life conceivable'[15] lodged deep in her memory, were brought vividly alive on the page near the end of her life in a remarkable memoir, 'Sketch of the Past', where St Ives is a 'windy, noisy, fishy, vociferous narrow-streeted town'[16], strange and romantic and quite unlike anywhere she had encountered. But as a very young child it was the random catalogue of sensory delights at Talland House, the now famous colour-and-sound memories of lying half awake in the nursery and hearing the waves on the shore, which were to have such a profound effect.

Her joyous reunion with this remote and enchanted corner of England in the summer of 1905, was tempered by the realisation that the centre of her childhood world was no longer hers. On approaching Talland House the Stephen children 'hung there like ghosts in the shade of the [escallonia] hedge & at the sound of footsteps we turned away.'[17] Virginia could never quite shrug off the allure of Cornwall. She remained in thrall to its great Atlantic rollers and craggy granite paths, returning throughout her life for long solitary walks or in the company of Leonard. It was Cornwall, Virginia's emotional bedrock, that helped shape some of her most enduring fiction, notably *To The Lighthouse*, and remained the yardstick by which all other landscapes were measured.

Between the death of her mother and her decision to rent a cottage in Sussex, Cornwall was replaced by a series of holidays taken in parts of the country quite unfamiliar to Virginia at a time which saw the emergence of a precocious literary talent. The first descriptive passages roughed out in her early journal, began to appear in the *Guardian* and *Times Literary Supplement* towards the end of 1904.

It is here and in her letters that Virginia's response to each new landscape suggests something of the stylistic verve that came to distinguish her fiction. Throughout these formative years her absorption in the physicality of place, the freedom to explore new territory and the process of writing down myriad new experiences also helped her cope with a succession of family bereavements.

An early indication of this growing confidence is contained in an exuberant letter to Emma Vaughan from Warboys rectory in the Fens where the Stephen family had chosen to spend the summer of 1899. The holiday had not started well, the intense heat, the flat terrain and a 'somewhat grim day of pleasure'[18] in the rain with her Stephen relatives induced in Virginia an air of melancholy. But towards the end of their stay she had begun to revel in this strange, ethereal land of Turneresque sunsets and dramatic cloudscapes:

> You don't see the sky until you live here. We have ceased to be dwellers on the earth. We are really made of clouds. We are mystical and dreamy and perform Fugues on the Harmonium .... I shall think it a test of friends for the future whether they can appreciate the Fen Country ... And there are people who think it dull and uninteresting!!!![19]

Virginia's response to the New Forest where, after Cornwall, the Stephen family stayed on several occasions, was altogether less enthusiastic: 'too benign & complaisant ... flaxen & florid, stately & ornamental'[20] she concluded on her last visit, Xmas 1906. With images of Haworth still fresh in her mind she longed for something altogether more raw and elemental – 'the dusky roll of some Northern moor, or the melancholy cliffs of Cornwall'[21]. Just beyond the Forest the 'wonderful rise and swell and fall' of the Wiltshire downs stretch away northwards. From here Virginia's Netherhampton House journal for the summer of 1903 consists entirely of short observational essays – Wilton sheep fair, the great house and the little town where 'the feudal spirit in England is not yet dead.'[22] These more assured pieces of reportage helped the author make sense of her surroundings. Salisbury Cathedral was all 'ancient loveliness & peace'[23] but, she cried, 'A bare hilltop would have pleased me better'[24] and turned instead to Stonehenge and the 'whole ocean of plain.'[25] This was her first real acquaintance with those same chalk hills that in Sussex were to become her constant companion and where 'If you lie on the earth somewhere you hear a sound like a vast breath'.[26]

The sense of freedom that came with each new landscape was yet more apparent a year later when Virginia was sent to recuperate in the Yorkshire

Dales following the death of her father. Here too the wintry, boulder-strewn crags above Settle appear like some vast petrified ocean – 'the moors rise in waves all round.'[27] Buoyed up by her trip to Haworth, she returned to the Dales in 1906 – her first holiday alone – where she found the austerity of this limestone country exciting and heroic. '[I] stride with gigantic strides over the wild moorside … I leap from crag to crag, and exalting in the air which buffets me … That is Stephen Brontëised'.[28]

Later that year Virginia and Vanessa found themselves in a 'strange, lonely kind of country'[29] on the Norfolk-Suffolk border. Here at Blo' Norton Hall where 'no sound what ever reaches your ear; the very light seems to filter through deep layers'[30] the two sisters enjoyed 'a kind of honeymoon'[31]. The hall, with its ancestral portraits and panelled rooms, had been occupied by generations of yeoman farmers and this sense of continuity inspired one of Virginia's 'beautiful, brilliant stories'[32], 'The Journal of Mistress Joan Martyn', and the moated house became a model for Pointz Hall in her last novel *Between The Acts*. Thetford too was much to her liking, somnambulant and medieval like an Italian town, but in truth Virginia was no antiquarian. Ruins like those at Glastonbury were often 'too clean, and too dilapidated'[33], and the bricks and mortar of history were of less interest to her than the mood and atmosphere of a place.

By the time she arrived on the edge of Romney Marsh the following summer (1907) Vanessa had married and although she and Clive Bell took a cottage in Rye 'of sister there is less than there used to be.'[34] This and the prospect of tea with Henry James coloured her impression of this gentrified little hilltop town which she soon found antiquated and exhausting and seemed intent on seeing the place swept clean of association, wandering out on the marsh in the evening. Her journal here contains a series of meditations on the dissolution of form that recall her Cornish essay 'A Walk by Night'. The mounds of Rye and Winchelsea 'make great soft blots on the landscape'[35] and after a day of wild weather 'the land all round was black & turbulent as the sea … it seemed as though the air itself was all broken & confused, a shattered medium …'[36]

From the time Virginia discovered the village of Firle near Lewes until her death thirty years later – half a lifetime – this corner of Sussex became her adopted country, an untainted landscape of bare chalk hills and water meadows that restored her health, nurtured her creativity and about which she became increasingly protective. Soon after their first meeting Virginia and Leonard stumbled upon a romantic house 'dropped beneath the Downs'[37] at the end of a walk along the ridgeway path and for the next few years the 'flawless beauty'[38] of Asheham provided Bloomsbury with its ideal rural retreat. The congenial company, the rhythm of country life and the seasonal pleasures of the garden induced in Virginia a sense of well-being essential to her recovery – 'Our ship rode so steady that one came to disbelieve in motion or the possibility of change … The loveliness of Asheham once again brimmed the cup & overflowed.'[39]

Since Cornwall Virginia's responses to landscape had necessarily been more impressionistic, the views panoramic and her attempts to commit them to paper a mixture of grand statement and painterly sketch. But in Sussex familiar scenes are transformed by weather and season; the diary she resumed in 1917 contains passages of close observation in the manner of Gilbert White's *Selborne*, a work she greatly admired. They are the product of a writer who knew her place, where the particular becomes universal: 'I remember lying on the side of a hollow, waiting for L. to come & mushroom, & seeing a red hare loping up the side & thinking suddenly "This is Earth Life".'[40]

When in 1919, the time came to vacate Asheham the pain of departure was relieved by the Woolf's decision to remain nearby and the proximity of Vanessa at Charleston. Their purchase of Monks House on the other side of the Ouse valley gave Virginia new territory to explore – up on the downs behind the village and along the river bank – and new perspectives on the place she had come to know and love. Here, despite the church bells, the school children and all the other distractions of village life, Virginia's daily routine soon reasserted itself and her diary is again lit by rapturous accounts of afternoon walks, the aftermath of autumnal gales and shafts of winter sunlight. While the garden was Leonard's domain the network of paths and farm tracks became her own forcing ground where stories began to take shape, where, according to Hermione Lee, the 'rhythm of walking gets into her sentences'[41] in one long, continuous process, where a walk on the South Downs is described:

… with that intense, sensual apprehension of landscape which she shared with [Gerard Manley] Hopkins. She watched this country 'haven' and worked in it, looked up from her book at it and walked through it … The landscape and the village were continually written into the diary and the letters – and there were stories and essays set in Sussex too.[42]

INTRODUCTION

When the Woolfs moved to Rodmell they also bought into the history of the village acquiring three naïve portraits of the Glazebrook family, millers by trade and 19th century owners of Monks House. Local residents, often unsentimentally depicted, appear in several short stories and although Virginia shrank from participation in village affairs she derived great satisfaction from a sense of community. From her writing hut beside the church her mind often drifted to the generations of parishioners buried beyond the garden wall and this feeling of continuity formed the basis of her final novel. *Between The Acts* is her *homage* to rural life and a celebration of place, where the deep roots of English history are embodied in a village pageant. Published a few months after her death it is also her farewell to Sussex.

Virginia Woolf was just the latest in a distinguished line of walking writers, most notably Hazlitt and the Romantic poets, who often covered long distances not just for the exercise or the scenery but as a way of freeing up thoughts – *solvitur ambulando* – 'you can sort it out by walking.' Others like Clare and Edward Thomas took to the field paths in an attempt to shake off the black dog of depression but for Virginia walking was both therapy and inspiration. Although her own prescriptive formula of Walking + Writing = Sanity served her well through much of her time in Sussex it was a fragile construct and one easily dislodged, especially when its very foundation was threatened.

Renewed ill-health during the terribly cold winter of 1940-41, an increasing sense of isolation and the stress induced by the publication of her biography of Roger Fry; all this with the noise of war and the constant threat of invasion conspired to hasten her death. Equally unsettling was the violation of her territory. She might have coped with those other metropolitan exiles, cultural pioneers of today's Glyndebourne set, but more disturbing was the creeping blight of development. Her beloved Asheham, abandoned and covered in chalk dust, had been despoiled by the cement works that rose from a huge quarry gouged out of the hillside. At Rodmell, by acquiring the adjacent meadow, the Woolfs were able to preserve their view of Mount Caburn but were powerless to halt the march of new houses that threatened to spill over the downs from 'the blasphemy of Peacehaven'[43]. Once again Virginia drew comfort from the onset of evening when 'the fields are redeemed. The freckle of red villas on the coast is washed over by a thin lucid lake of brown air …'[44]

From the sound of those waves breaking at St Ives to the peace of Asheham, 'very like living at the bottom of the sea being here'[45], and '[t]he Downs breaking their wave'[46], watery images run through Virginia's writing. Moorlands become heaving oceans, hills exist only to provide a view of the sea, preferably the Atlantic, and at dusk the land becomes liquid as it sinks beneath a rising tide of darkness. A few months before Virginia's death an enemy bomb had blown a hole in the Ouse embankment flooding the whole valley to her evident pleasure. When the end came she chose the unforgiving waters of that same river beside which she had walked so often and where 'the human spirit immersed at the end in the spirit of place.'[47]

I
CORNWALL

Why am I so incredibly and incurably romantic about Cornwall?

In many ways Sir Leslie Stephen conformed to the archetypal Victorian patriarch. His striking appearance and boundless energy had equipped him well for life at Eton and at Cambridge his appetite for hard work and athletic prowess was much admired by fellow undergraduates. He soon became a competent rower, an accomplished Alpine climber and joint instigator of an informal walking group known as the Sunday Tramps. His love of hiking and the natural world were two of the 'manly' traits inherited by his younger daughter Virginia and led, in 1881, to his discovery of Talland House, St Ives, at the end of one of his great walking holidays 'down at the very toe-nail of England.'[1]

The house, named most probably after the Cornish village near Polperro, was a modest villa set off with geometrically patterned bay windows and a wrought iron balcony on the roof that Virginia found so appealing, and it suited the requirements of a growing family with servants. It also offered unrivalled views out across the bay and a choice of sandy coves where the Stephen children could play in safety under the watchful eye of nanny, leaving their father free to explore the peninsula. St Ives was still an unspoilt fishing town that, despite a long, arduous journey, could now be reached by train from London. Talland House was part of the Tregenna Castle estate purchased by the Great Western Railway Company as a prestigious hotel when the branch line was opened in 1874, and Leslie Stephen managed to acquire a lease on the property that became the family's summer residence each year until his wife Julia's death in 1895.

Sir Leslie Stephen
(1832-1904)

Talland House, c.1900

The arrival of the branch line from St Erth came at just the right time to transform St Ives into a coastal resort of some distinction. Its staple industries were in decline – the pilchards had already forsaken the bay and the tin mines in the hills above were no longer profitable. Among the first itinerant painters to be seen about the narrow streets were Whistler and Sickert who spent several weeks working in the old fishing quarter of Downlong during the winter of 1883-84. The discovery of St Ives saw the conversion of redundant sail lofts into studios along Porthmear Beach and the growth of a renowned artists' colony. The Stephen family was part of this first gentle wave of summer visitors but for Virginia, recalling those early childhood holidays near the end of her life, the place was unknown, unspoilt and had remained unchanged for centuries:

> ... a scramble of granite houses crusting the slope ... Many houses had a flight of steps, with a railing leading to the door. The walls were thick blocks of granite built to stand the sea storms. They were splashed with a wash the colour of Cornish cream; ... [the town] had no architecture; no arrangement. The market place was a jagged cobbled open place; the Church was on one side; built of granite, ageless, like the houses ...[2]

For Virginia its stark, uncompromising beauty was the perfect antidote to all those images of picturesque thatch and antiquated brickwork of which she had grown tired. The 'only attempt that the town made at ornament'[3] took the

Great Western Railway poster

shape of the Malakoff, an octagonal platform overlooking the harbour, popular with retired fishermen. Otherwise this steep-sided, gull-haunted, 'windy, noisy, fishy, vociferous, narrow-streeted town; the colour of a mussel or a limpet'[4] inhabited by mischievous urchins and 'innumerable cats with their fishbones in their mouths'[5], was a world away from genteel Sussex.

Preparations at Hyde Park Gate for the annual expedition to St Ives presented something of a logistical nightmare before the whole family were assembled on the platform ready to board the Cornish Express accompanied by their cook, a parlour maid, a governess and a mountain of luggage sufficient for a ten week holiday. Compared to the freedom of St Ives, where the children were allowed to scramble among the rocks or take a boat out in the bay, life in London seemed dull in the extreme – 'non-being lay thick over those years'[6] – alleviated by twice-daily walks in Kensington Gardens where Virginia derived some little comfort from sailing her Cornish lugger on the pond. The relief experienced by all the Stephen children as the 10.15am pulled out of Paddington station was almost palpable. Towards the end of an exhausting nine hour journey the sense of anticipation grew with each succeeding mile until, with the first glimpse of St Ives at the far end of the bay, the family squeezed into a carriage on the branch line at St Erth ready to complete the last stage of their yearly migration.

Back Road East, Downlong

ENGLISH HOURS

For Virginia, on arrival at Talland House, the familiar click of the garden gate opened up a world of sensory delights. The grounds, tumbling downhill towards the beach, were sub-divided by sweet-smelling escallonia hedges into a series of small, intimate spaces, each with its own designated purpose, its own secrets and imaginative possibilities. In addition to the more functional kitchen garden, the strawberry beds and the cricket lawn in which

Barnoon Hill, c.1900
popular among artists

Virginia confirmed her reputation as a demon bowler, there was the Love Corner where the children overheard Leo Maxse propose to Kitty Lushington, the spreading elm trees where their neighbour George Meredith read his poems to their mother, Julia Stephen, and the rubbish heap, home to the evil spirits Beccage and Hollywinks. Most popular of all was Lookout Point, a grassy hummock projecting out over the boundary wall. From here the children would keep watch on the railway signal, the fall of which heralded the arrival of guests to a household already bursting at the seams. As they grew older the Stephen children and their cousins were squeezed into the attic space while visitors spilled over onto floor mats or made do with a selection of camp beds. Virginia's godfather, the poet, critic and American Ambassador, James Lowell, often braved the spartan comforts of Talland House but another regular guest, Henry James, preferred the relative luxury and elevated position of the Tregenna Castle Hotel as a base for long tramps over the Penwith peninsula with Leslie Stephen as his silent companion. For Virginia, too, it was the unrivalled view out across the bay that kept her enthralled.

Virginia (left) and Vanessa at Talland House, 1894

St Ives' harbour before the construction of Wharf Road in 1922

... a large Bay, many curved, edged with a slip of sand, with green sand hills behind; and the curves flowed in and out of the two black rocks at one end of which stood the black and white tower of the Lighthouse; and at the other end, Hayle river made a blue vein across the sand, and stakes, on which always a gull sat, marked the channel ... This great flowing basin of water was always changing in colour; it was deep blue; emerald green; purple and then stormy grey and white crested. There was a great coming and going of ships ... Most usually, it was a Haines steamer, with a red or white band round the funnel, going to Cardiff for coal. In rough weather, sometimes one would wake to find the whole bay full of ships ... little tramp steamers mostly ... once a battle ship ...[7]

Hick's Court, Downlong

Thanks largely to the energy and sense of duty displayed by Virginia's mother, the family contributed in some small way to the life of the community. Each year Julia resumed her charitable works with regular visits to the town's more unfortunate inhabitants and, following her death, the society she established was named the Julia Prinsep Stephen Nursing Association. Contact with local people was otherwise more perfunctory, in the shape of their washer-woman, Alice Curnow, or Mrs Adams, who climbed the hill each week to deposit live lobsters on the kitchen table. Charlie Pearce, the blind town crier, was another local character recalled with affection by Virginia. One of his most keenly-awaited ceremonial functions was to announce the forthcoming regatta, held in the bay each August, when large crowds thronged the harbour walls and gathered on the Malakoff to watch the spectacle unfold. 'It was a very gay sight, with flags flying, the guns firing, the boats sailing, and the swimmers plunging...'[8]

In the company of their father the Stephen children would often venture beyond the town; to woods nearby known to them as Fairyland, where they balanced on the boundary wall and peered down into its depths – 'It smelt of oak apples; it was dark, damp, silent, mysterious.'[9] Up on the hills behind St Ives they negotiated the uncertain terrain of Halsetown Bog in search of the rare maiden-hair fern or scrambled through gorse and heather to the top of Trencrom (their Trick Robin), a local beauty spot where they loved to climb the Loggan stone and set it rocking. Here 'perhaps the hollow in the rough lichened surface was for the victim's blood.'[10] Looking back on these childhood adventures and possibly with this image in mind, Virginia declared that she had come increasingly to begrudge the regular Sunday hikes: 'Father must have one of us to go out with him, Mother insisted. Too much obsessed with his health, with his pleasures, she was too willing, as I think now, to sacrifice us to him.'[11]

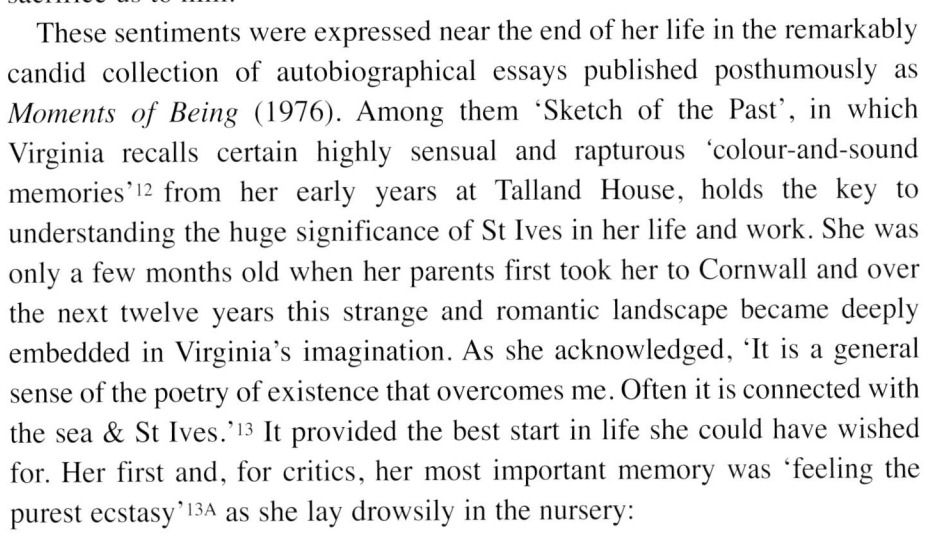

Ellen Eldridge and delivery boy at Talland House, c.1892

These sentiments were expressed near the end of her life in the remarkably candid collection of autobiographical essays published posthumously as *Moments of Being* (1976). Among them 'Sketch of the Past', in which Virginia recalls certain highly sensual and rapturous 'colour-and-sound memories'[12] from her early years at Talland House, holds the key to understanding the huge significance of St Ives in her life and work. She was only a few months old when her parents first took her to Cornwall and over the next twelve years this strange and romantic landscape became deeply embedded in Virginia's imagination. As she acknowledged, 'It is a general sense of the poetry of existence that overcomes me. Often it is connected with the sea & St Ives.'[13] It provided the best start in life she could have wished for. Her first and, for critics, her most important memory was 'feeling the purest ecstasy'[13A] as she lay drowsily in the nursery:

It is of hearing the waves breaking, one, two, one, two, and sending a splash of water over the beach; and then breaking, one, two, one, two, behind a yellow blind. It is of hearing the blind draw its little acorn across the floor as the wind blew the blind out.[14]

On top of this and then mingled with it was the clamour of rooks in the elm trees. 'The quality of the air ... seemed to suspend sound, to let it sink down slowly, as if it were caught in a blue gummy veil. The rooks cawing is part of the waves breaking –'[15] Later, in the garden, where the apple trees stretched away downhill, it 'gave off a murmur of bees; the apples were red and gold; there were also pink flowers; and grey and silver leaves. The buzz, the croon, the smell, all seemed to press voluptuously against some membrane ...'[16]

These memories, reeled in and rearranged on the page, were 'an incongruous miscellaneous catalogue, little corks that mark a sunken net.'[17] Re-lived more intensely than events of the previous day, these moments of being appeared to have an independent existence, but they were not always entirely pleasurable. Most days at Talland House, and throughout Virginia's life, were filled with what she called 'this cotton wool, this non-being.'[18] Then, for no apparent reason, some incident recalled vividly would come crashing through her brain. In the middle of a fight with Thoby on the lawn she once stopped abruptly, overcome with 'a feeling of hopeless sadness.'[19] On another occasion, seeing a plant by the front door inextricably part of the earth, she felt she had made a discovery, that a pattern of existence lurked behind the cotton wool. At times, walking by moonlight in the garden she would be struck down by a feeling of absolute despair, unable to pass a certain apple tree that was somehow connected with the suicide of a local St Ives resident. More traumatic was the animal face that would suddenly appear over her shoulder in the hall mirror, a disturbing symbol of the disgust she felt for her own body, compounded by the sense of violation at the hands of her elder half brother, Gerald Duckworth, who had 'interfered' with her outside the dining room.

Throughout her career Virginia reworked incidents from childhood and family life into her fiction, drawing heavily on memories of St Ives to create scenes in *The Voyage Out*, *The Waves* and *Jacob's Room* where the white cottages are set down firmly on Cornwall's cliffs – 'the garden grows gorse more readily than cabbages'[20] – and where, astride legendary granite boulders, tourists can enjoy the prospect of Gurnard's Head. *To The Lighthouse*, in which Vanessa is the model for the artist Lily Briscoe, and the Ramsays are revealing portraits of her parents, is Virginia's most autobiographical work of

Dust Jacket design
Vanessa Bell, 1927

fiction. This, together with the number of friends and local residents who appear as minor characters, may help explain the author's decision to locate the novel on a remote Hebridean island. Here she could safely recreate the ebb and flow of life at Talland House including the now famous boat trip to Godrevy Lighthouse, the idea for which, according to Virginia's *Hyde Park Gate News*, came from an invitation to her and brother Thoby 'as Freeman the boatman said that there was a perfect tide and wind for going there.'[21]

The lighthouse from Godrevy Point

Although it was eventually the death of Virginia's mother that precipitated the disposal of Talland House, Leslie Stephen had become increasingly concerned about the cost of educating his two sons and 'ominous hints reached the nursery that the grown ups talked of leaving St Ives.'[22] With the arrival of the railway, rows of terrace houses had begun to spread rapidly uphill from the old fishing town and the year before Julia's death it was the appearance of the 'great square oatmeal coloured hotel'[23] (the Porthminster) on the slopes below Talland that threatened the view and persuaded Virginia's parents to sell the lease. Over the intervening years the grounds have been drastically reduced as first the orchard and then the glasshouses were sold off to satisfy the same insatiable appetite for a view of the bay. The house too has inevitably undergone a series of alterations, most noticeably the removal of the original staircase and the replacement of the little attic windows and rooftop balcony with one long, continuous dormer. Despite the holiday flats that now separate the property from the beach Talland House, with its escallonia hedge, its elegant French windows and bedroom balconies, is in many ways still recognisably the place Virginia found so enchanting all those years before, as the reader slips effortlessly into the world of *Jacob's Room*:

... the grey-green garden, and among the pear-shaped leaves of the escallonia fishing-boats seemed caught and suspended. A sailing-ship slowly drew past the women's backs. Two or three figures crossed the terrace hastily in the dusk ... Like oars rowing now this side, now that, were the sentences that came now here, now there, from either side of the table.[24]

The coast west of St Ives with Gurnard's Head in the distance

Following years of self-imposed exile Virginia's return to Cornwall in August 1905 was an emotional reunion with the place that throughout her youth had been more like home than anywhere else. This ancient, boulder-strewn country of rocky headlands, zephyrus sea breezes and wild Atlantic rollers had cast its spell all those years before and she now found herself drawn back almost every year like some exotic migrant to hover about the scenes of her childhood happiness. Striding out over the moors or along the craggy coastal paths Virginia came to haunt the old familiar landmarks of this most remote corner of England, an enchanted landscape by which all others were to be measured:

> Why am I so incredibly & incurably romantic about Cornwall? One's past, I suppose: I see children running in the garden. ... The sound of the sea at night. And now I go back "bringing my sheaves" – well, Leonard, & almost 40 years of life, all built on that, permeated by that: how much so I could never explain. And in reality it is very beautiful. I shall go down to Treveal & look at the sea – old waves that have been breaking precisely so these thousand years.[25]

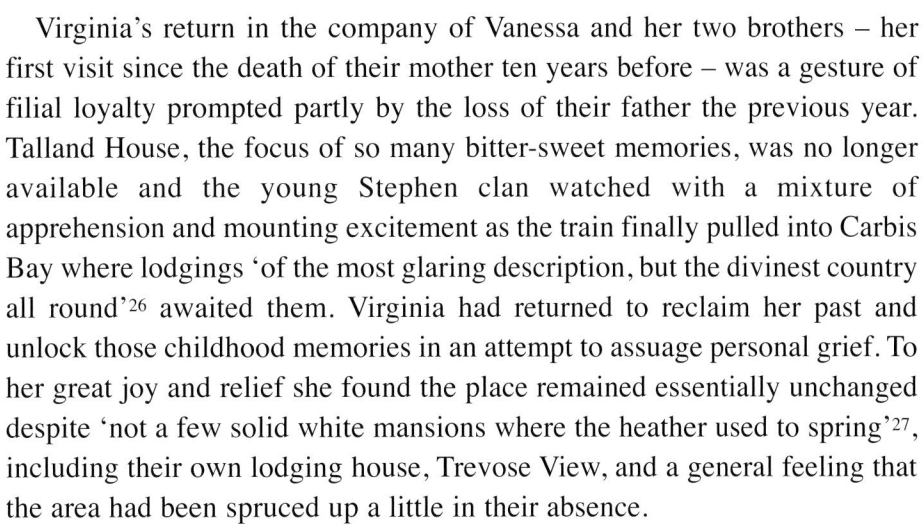

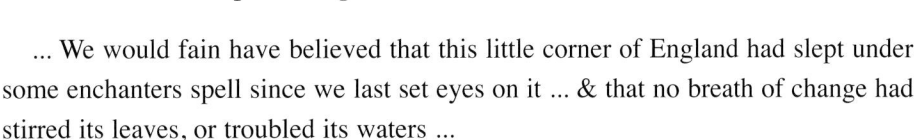

Virginia's return in the company of Vanessa and her two brothers – her first visit since the death of their mother ten years before – was a gesture of filial loyalty prompted partly by the loss of their father the previous year. Talland House, the focus of so many bitter-sweet memories, was no longer available and the young Stephen clan watched with a mixture of apprehension and mounting excitement as the train finally pulled into Carbis Bay where lodgings 'of the most glaring description, but the divinest country all round'[26] awaited them. Virginia had returned to reclaim her past and unlock those childhood memories in an attempt to assuage personal grief. To her great joy and relief she found the place remained essentially unchanged despite 'not a few solid white mansions where the heather used to spring'[27], including their own lodging house, Trevose View, and a general feeling that the area had been spruced up a little in their absence.

Talland House today

> ... We would fain have believed that this little corner of England had slept under some enchanters spell since we last set eyes on it ... & that no breath of change had stirred its leaves, or troubled its waters ...
>
> Ah, how strange it was, then, to watch the familiar shapes of land & sea unroll themselves once more, as though a magicians hand had raised the curtain that hung between us, & to see once more the silent but palpable forms ...[28]

On their arrival at Trevose View it was already dusk, a time of day that seemed only to enhance the sense of unreality and adventure. Once unpacked they set out round the headland to Porthminster Bay and soon found themselves on the driveway that led up to Talland House where they peered nervously through a gap in the escallonia hedge upon a scene that made Virginia's heart race.

... But yet, as we knew well, we could go no further, if we advanced the spell was broken. The lights were not our lights, the voices were the voices of strangers. We hung there like ghosts in the shade of the hedge, & at the sound of footsteps we turned away.[29]

The voices were those of the artist Thomas Millie Dow and his family and it was with some trepidation that, later in the holiday, Virginia and the others accepted an invitation to take tea. In August 1905, as dawn broke on the day

Knill's Monument, c.1905

after their arrival, Virginia looked out across the bay and was at once reassured that the events of the previous day had not all been a dream. Out on the hills above the bay 'among the fields of paradise, among Gods'[30] as

Granite cattle grid on the Church Path near Zennor

she wrote enthusiastically to her friend, Emma Vaughan, the Stephen children revelled in the grandeur of the landscape, striking south along the old trackways to Trencrom, the conical hill that had once been the destination of so many Sunday walks. Here from the top of its ancient ramparts, they could take in the view beyond Hayle Harbour to Godrevy and then south to St Michael's Mount and as far round as the Lizard; another rocky promontory with its own lighthouse. More surprising and the source of greater satisfaction was the discovery of familiar details – way-markers along their path that might so easily have disappeared; the dunghill in the yard at Peacock's Farm, the plank bridge across the stream, and those projecting blocks of granite placed conveniently to enable travellers to negotiate each stone wall.

In the coming days Virginia slipped easily into her preferred routine of solitary afternoon walks, greeting familiar landmarks like long lost friends so that 'the map of the land becomes solid in my brain.'[31] She found this process of reclaiming her territory exhilarating in all weathers; in driving rain or the sweet scents of an August day with everything bathed in the warm glow of 'an amber coloured medium'.[32] At Knill's Monument, a granite pyramid erected in 1782 above Carbis Bay to commemorate a reformed smuggler-turned-lawyer who became mayor of St Ives, even the disorientating effects of 'dense vapours'[33] failed to dampen Virginia's delight as she continued to revel in her surroundings.

> The impetuous sweep of the large bay [St Ives], curving round so that it half completes the circle, gives one an impression of beautifully curbed vitality; again in hollowing the three smaller bays [Porthminster, Carbis and Lelant] in the flank of the large one she must, one would think, have had an eye to the fair proportion of the whole. They do not interfere with the single large impression; but they add something original; & unexpected ... Lelant Bay, is in some respects the loveliest of the three. It makes the rounded corner of the large Bay; but the sweep of white sands is intersected by the Hayle river, which draws a blue line down to the sea. ... At ebb tide in the evening the stretch of sands here is vast & melancholy; the waves spread themselves one over lapping the other in thin fan shaped layers of water; ... The slope of the beach gleams as though laid with a film of mother o' pearl where the sea has been, & a row of sea gulls sits on the skirts of the repeating wave. The pallor of the sandhills makes the scene yet more ghostly, but the beautiful sights are often melancholy & very lonely.[34]

While planning this holiday Virginia and the others had promised themselves a trip round the bay and on a clear morning soon after their arrival they set off down to the harbour where, at that time of the year, a fishing boat could be hired for the day. But as the sun rose the breeze dropped and the vessel made little headway. The ferryman who was soon forced to take up his oars was also obliged to entertain his inquisitive guests with 'discourse of the sea'[35] when 'a sudden exclamation of porpoises'[36] appeared alongside the boat to the delight of its passengers and the relief of the boatman who was fast running through his repertoire of shipwreck tales. More significantly, as he explained, the presence of porpoises meant the early arrival of pilchards. That same evening people began to gather on the headland that separates Porthminster from Carbis Bay as the seine boats lay in wait below but it was a few days later before the cry of 'pilchards in the bay' rang out. Then the buzz of excitement spread quickly through Downlong, the town's fishing quarter beside the harbour, transforming a dull, misty day into one of intense activity.

This is Sain Fishery that used to be, Alfred Wallis, the St Ives fisherman-painter

The pilchard industry had been a mainstay of the local economy throughout the 19th century but increased foreign competition and changes in the pattern of fish migration meant that by the time Virginia recorded the onset of the season so vividly in her journal, the whole business was already in terminal decline. This only served to increase the sense of expectation as Virginia, Vanessa and their brothers rushed down to the lookout house on

Porthminster Point where appointed 'hewers' were orchestrating the whole dramatic operation. Seine boats, gathered 'like long black insects with rows of legs'[37] waiting to shoot their nets, were being manoeuvred into position by megaphone instructions from the headland as 'a certain faint purple shadow'[38], the first sizeable shoal of pilchards, entered the bay. Soon after another shoal appeared further east and rival boats from Carbis Bay set out in pursuit. By the time the first shoal had been netted Virginia and the others had managed to find a boat in the harbour that would take them out to where the 'water within seethed with fish. It was packed with iridescent fish, gleaming silver & purple, leaping in the air; lashing their tails, sending up showers of scales.'[39] As they watched, fishermen plunged their baskets repeatedly into the 'bubbling mass'[40] until their holds were full and the catch landed on the quayside. Here another crowd of men, women and children were ready to begin the arduous task of gutting, salting and packing the harvest ready for export.

Packing fish near the Sloop Inn, 1904

Days later they ventured further afield in search of 'more substantial beauties'[41] and hired a brake to take them along the tortuous coast to Lands End. Even at that time their enjoyment of this romantic conjunction of rocky outcrops and surging foam was compromised by the arrival, at intervals, of car-borne tourists intent on admiring the same impressive view bathed in the golden light of a late September afternoon. On the return journey via

Penzance they headed for St Buryan's, a weather-beaten granite village, whose tall, 'perfectly unornamented'[42] church tower beckoned for miles across a bleak, pagan landscape of stone circles and megalithic tombs. On arrival they found its treasures – most notably a sumptuously carved medieval screen – hidden away behind locked doors and had to console themselves with a somewhat mutilated Celtic cross in the churchyard.

Towards the end of their six week stay Virginia found the eye eventually tired of 'unstable waters'[43] and so they decided to strike inland. 'There is a certain austere dignity among these hills although they are not actually beautiful'.[44] Their destination was Castle Dinas, another fragmented hill fort about five miles south west across rocky moorland in the very heart of this ancient landscape. From the summit, marked by a folly-cum-lookout known as Roger's Tower, the view encompasses the whole peninsula from shore to shore. '[L]ittle visits to the country people in their lonely farms'[45] had become an integral part of their walking tours and, on descending Castle Dinas, Virginia found the need to rest and quench her thirst provided a rare opportunity to converse with local people and observe the way they lived. Almost invariably she found them courteous and hospitable if, at times, a little wary of such well spoken and oddly attired strangers.

The weird nocturnal sounds and murky shapes encountered during a late evening walk always held a peculiar fascination for Virginia. Having got as far as Gurnard's Head, a rocky headland just beyond Zennor that, years later, she rediscovered with Leonard, the young party set out on the return journey. Led by Adrian they left the road and entered a 'vast trackless country,'[46]

Crucifixion scene
Celtic cross, St. Buryan

> ... Once in this strange pilgrimage we groped our way through a farm-yard, where the shapes of dim cattle loomed large, & a great lantern swung an unsteady disk of light across our faces. The voice of the farmer bidding us good night recalled us for a moment to the cheerful land of substance ... We stumbled across fields which swam in dusky vapours ... Now we had come to the lights in the valley ... Night was weighing heavily on this little village; all was silent though not asleep ... how intense that light after the vague immensity of the air; we were like creatures lately winged that have been caught & caged.[47]

Here, as elsewhere in *A Passionate Apprentice,* Virginia used her journal to draft an early version of an essay; in this case entitled 'A Walk by Night' which appeared later that same year in the *Guardian* (28th Dec. 1905).

Virginia was soon back in St Ives – in April 1908 – sharing a lodging house in Draycott Terrace, close to Talland House, a place full of noisy children with 'a confidential man'[48] and his family. Awaiting the arrival of Vanessa and Clive Bell with their new baby, Julian, she busied herself with a review of the *Life of Delane*, a depressing but necessary task for the *Cornhill Magazine* alleviated by long hikes inland over the hills with her dog Gurth. The following year, while walking through Regent's Park on Christmas Eve she was suddenly struck by '... how absurd it was to stay in London, with Cornwall going on all the time. ...'[49] Half an hour later she had bought a ticket and was sitting in the Penzance train with only Lady Hester Stanhope's *Memoirs* for company. At St Erth she changed trains as usual but instead of St Ives decided on a whim to alight at Lelant and booked into a deserted hotel overlooking the Hayle estuary with Godrevy lighthouse just visible at the far end of the bay. Here she revelled in the solitude, took long walks along the sand and climbed Trencrom Hill behind the village where a thick sea mist deprived her of the glorious views to be had from this local beauty spot. By day she was entertained by tales of wrecks and drowned sailors gleaned from her landlady and the ferryman who rowed her across to the dunes on the far side of the river. In the evening she listened to the sounds of carol singing that drifted in through her window on the mild sea air.

At the end of June 1910 Virginia was admitted to a private nursing home in Twickenham suffering from nervous exhaustion. Six weeks later her doctor decided that recuperation would be assisted by the sea air and regular exercise

Lelant c.1915. The hotel, now the Badger Inn, is on the right

of a walking holiday in Cornwall, and on August 16th she set out with the proprietor of Burghley Park, Jean Thomas, a woman whose company she had come to enjoy: 'She has a charming nature; rather whimsical, and even sensual.'[50] A few days later and Virginia was writing enthusiastically to fellow Bloomsberry, Saxon Sydney-Turner, from Tintagel: 'Really, there is no place quite so beautiful as Cornwall – in spite of the inconvenience caused by several passionate lovers'[51] disporting themselves on the coastal path. She even felt well enough to add hurriedly: 'I hope you have had no more fits.'[52] Three weeks later near the end of their tour she was fully recovered and writing to Clive Bell from Gurnard's Head at the end of a day spent walking along the cliffs from St Just:

... among the most remarkable moors, among barrows, British villages, stone maidens, and beehive huts. If it weren't for the excitability of geese at night, [they were staying at Berryman's Farm] this would be the place I should like to live in.[53]

Gurnard's Head

This dream was almost realised some years later when Katherine Mansfield alerted Virginia to a row of cottages at Tregerthen on the Church Path between Zennor and St Ives that DH Lawrence was hoping to sub-let. The proposition, made in March 1919, was particularly attractive because it provided the Woolfs with a ready solution to the immediate problem of moving from Asheham. Virginia, who was enthusiastic from the start, thought they could keep a toe-hold in Sussex by renting a cottage at Firle. Lawrence, on hearing of their interest, wrote to Leonard: 'The houses are planted on the hillside, slap above the sea, which is about ten minutes, down the fields. It is beautiful, I think, and as lonely as necessary.'[54] The landscape would always be beautiful but during the war local people had become increasingly suspicious of the bearded prophet and his German wife.

Lanyon Quoit, Madron

The outcry that had greeted the publication of *The Rainbow* in 1915 prompted Lawrence to consider emigrating to Florida where his idea for a Utopian community could be tested but, having gained exemption from military service because of his tuberculosis, he stumbled upon Higher Tregerthen while staying at the Tinner's Arms in Zennor. The notion that his Rananim might flourish in the stony terrain of north Cornwall was always debatable but, once installed, Lawrence set about persuading Middleton Murry and Katherine Mansfield to leave France and join them in the empty cottage next door. '... one sees infinite Atlantic, all peacock-mingled colours, and the gorse is sunshine itself ...'[55]. Shortly after their arrival the Murrys began to question the wisdom of their decision. Katherine's response to the harsh environment was decidedly unenthusiastic. 'It is not really a nice place. It is so full of huge stones.'[56] Life with the Lawrences was an equally bumpy ride and it was not long before the two couples had fallen out. The men were sworn blood brothers but when Lawrence's amorous overtures were not reciprocated he launched into a bilious attack on Murry. 'I hate your love, I hate it ... you're an obscene bug sucking my life away.'⁵⁷ All this, the lambs eating the lettuces and the howling wind; in short the occupational hazards that beset most rural communities, utopian or otherwise, was quite enough for the Murrys who sought refuge on the more sheltered slopes of Cornwall's south coast, leaving Lawrence to pour the experience into *Women in Love*.

Village Street, Zennor, Sven Berlin, 1947,

These personal dramas were played out against a backdrop of a country at war; the couple were thought to be spies, a suspicion given added weight by the news that Frieda was related to Germany's flying ace, the Red Baron. The cottages were raided and the Lawrences unceremoniously ordered out of

Cornwall. Not surprisingly Lawrence was anxious to dispose of his tenancy but Virginia, fearful that the cottages might be taken, wrote directly to the owner, Captain Short, and secured all three for £15 p.a. each. Sounding more like a property tycoon than a published author her letter to Janet Case in July 1919 neatly summarised the Woolfs' portfolio and their dilemma:

> ... Did Leonard tell you how we bought a house in Lewes, and then saw one we liked better at Rodmell, and so bought that, and have now sold the first house, and have only 3 cottages in Cornwall, and Asheham, and the house at Rodmell and Hogarth House to live in? [58]

Eagle's Nest above the Lawrence/Woolf cottages, Higher Tregerthen

Realising they couldn't possibly hang on to them the Woolfs tried to share their Cornish cottages with the painter Mark Arnold-Forster and his wife, formerly Ka Cox, but the suggestion never came to anything. The cottages were re-let and the Arnold-Forsters, who were looking for something more spacious and equipped with a bathroom, eventually found Eagle's Nest nearby, perched on a rocky outcrop above Tregerthen. The Woolfs, having relinquished their cottages, were glad still to have a base in this part of Cornwall. They paid their first visit in March 1921 but soon discovered that the spectacular views from Eagle's Nest came at a price. It 'stands up too much of a castle-boardinghouse to be a pleasant object; but considering the winds, firm roots are needed.'[59] They found the house so exposed and cold that they soon retreated to lodgings at Poniou on the far side of Zennor. Here Virginia attempted to nail a series of precise, interconnected images of the Cornish landscape, consigning lengthy descriptive passages to her diary, re-working the more attractive pieces into long entertaining letters, a form of translation she often adopted. The letter to Saxon Sydney-Turner, written on Gurnard's Head, is typical:

…We step out into the June sunshine, past mounds of newly sprung gorse, bright yellow and smelling of nuts, over a grey stone wall, so along a cart track scattered with granite to a cliff, beneath which is the sea, of the consistency of innumerable plovers eggs where they turn grey green semi transparent. However when the waves curl over they are more like emeralds, and then the spray at the top is blown back like a mane – an old simile doubtless, but rather a good one. … the seals may bob up, first looking like logs, then like naked old men, with tridents for tails. I'm not sure though that the beauty of the country isn't its granite hills … But the last night walking through Zennor the granite was – amazing, … half transparent, … All the village dogs were waiting outside the church, and the strange Cornish singing inside …[60]

As Virginia's love for Cornwall became more intense and more eloquently expressed so she bristled in equal measure as her precious countryside became appropriated by unsavoury newcomers – 'most of the cottages are inhabited by the riff raff of Chelsea'[61]. She was even prepared to purchase a cottage with four acres of moorland on Tregerthen Hill for Sydney-Turner, Belgravia's opera-loving recluse, a rather fanciful ruse to prevent it falling into the wrong hands. Here she pictured him tending his cow, warming himself over a peat fire, '… and the sublimity of your thoughts, reading Greek in the morning, and Latin in the evening would in time come to invest your lodging with radiance.'[62] She complained to Ka Cox: 'I'm afraid Cornwall is becoming a little too exalted'[63] with Bertrand Russell at Penzance and the Manning Sanders at Sennen Cove, a colony of writers and artists joined some years later by Mary Butts whose Dorset novels were to be rejected by the Hogarth Press (see Chapt.XI). Virginia reserved her most poisonous invective for the young theosophist and his wife who had moved into 'their' Tregerthen cottages and may well have been vetted by Lawrence himself. Her letter to Lytton Strachey begins with reference to a pair of adders curled round her ankles on Gurnard's Head before developing the reptilian theme:

> ... the theosophist ... lives on nuts from Selfridges, and a few vegetables, and has visions, and wears boots with soles like slabs of beef and an orange tie; and then his wife crept out of her hole, all blue, with orange hair, and cryptic ornaments, serpents, you know, swallowing their tails in token of eternity, round her neck.[64]

Ruinous granite farm buildings on Penwith

The Woolfs spent Christmas 1926 with the Arnold-Forsters and were happy to use Eagle's Nest as a base for touring the peninsular but the intense cold and an endless stream of visitors curtailed their stay and coloured Virginia's impression of their host. She considered Will 'a water-blooded waspish little man, all on edge, vain, peevish, nervous. Ka is matronly, but substantial.'[65] Ten years later when Virginia was suffering from nervous exhaustion on completing *The Years*, Leonard considered another holiday in Cornwall would restore her health as it had so often in the past. They stayed once more with the Arnold-Forsters and later 'at this absurd hotel near the detestable town of Falmouth.'[66] Writing to Vita Sackville-West near the end of what was almost certainly her last visit to Cornwall, the place had clearly lost none of its magic despite her growing impatience with its new inhabitants:

... My word – what a country! Why do we ever spend any part of our short lives in Sussex Kent or London? We dribble from bay to bay, and have discovered an entirely lonely virgin country – not a bungalow – only gulls foot prints on sand. Here and there a castle, and an old man fishing in his river with the sea breaking behind ilex groves, and a rim of green hill.[67]

Sennen Cove, Cornwall, Dame Laura Knight, 1926

II
THE BORDERS

A landscape that is to me the loveliest in the world

In September 1897 near the end of the Stephen's annual retreat to the country, staying on this occasion at Painswick rectory in the Cotswolds, their friend Jack Hills posed the question 'shall we go to Corby'[1]? This was not a reference to the market town of that name, but to the grand country house in Cumbria where his parents lived. The matter was soon settled by Leslie Stephen and after a brief return to Hyde Park Gate to enable Virginia and Vanessa to replenish their wardrobe, the two sisters found themselves aboard the Euston to Glasgow express, bound for a remote outpost near the Scottish border. This, their first trip north, was long and uneventful and involved changing trains for

Corby Castle

the village of Wetherall, some four miles east of Carlisle. From here it was a short distance upstream to Great Corby and its 'castle' set in beautiful countryside above the wooded slopes of a swift-flowing river: '– a river quite different from our beloved Thames – it is most fiery and excitable –'[2].

The river Eden below Corby Castle

The castle, which had begun life in more troubled times as a pele tower, had been considerably enlarged and domesticated by the Howard family in the late 17th century and again in the early 19th century. When Virginia arrived she found 'a great red square country house'[3] fashioned from the local sandstone, pedimented and porticoed in the Greek Revival style. It was set in landscaped grounds dotted with temples and a summer house with its own cascade, an arcadian pleasure ground spread out in the Vale of Eden of a kind more usually associated with the gentle contours of southern England she had just vacated. The house was disconcertingly grand and overpowering with a huge entrance hall, a maze of principal rooms, a gallery and servants at every turn. In her only surviving letter from Corby, addressed to her brother Thoby, Virginia complained: 'I have never been in the midst of such gorgeosity in the whole of my long life. ... We have long long dinners – seven courses – and everything is very stately and uncomfortable.'[4] The place was presided over by Jack's mother, an unpleasant woman dressed in black who leased Corby Castle from the ancestral Dukes of Norfolk and who was insufferably proud of both the size of her retinue and her aristocratic connections. Mrs Hills was among the first of many upper middle class ladies who made Virginia feel acutely inadequate, a woman she soon came to detest.

The Cascade, Corby Castle

Left to their own devices the two sisters might have chosen to explore the river bank where, on the far side, beyond the red sandstone gatehouse of Wetherall Priory, was a group of man-made caves traditionally associated with St Constantine. But Virginia (aged 15) and Vanessa (18) were considered too young to stray far from Mrs Hills' piercing black eyes. The day after their arrival was a Sunday, a day 'very dismal and strange'[5] when they were allowed out in the morning to play by the river but with Jack in attendance. Otherwise they passed the day bored and neglected and in the evening Virginia wrote despairingly '– everything is miserable & lonely. Why did we ever come – Jack does not very much want us.'[6]

ENGLISH HOURS

The answer was not simply that he preferred salmon fishing as an escape from family responsibilities. Just below the surface lurked a recent trauma that clouded Virginia's response to the place and compounded her gloomy state of mind. At the beginning of the year, after a long courtship, Jack had finally married her half-sister and surrogate mother Stella Duckworth, but just three months later she had died suddenly of peritonitis leaving him devastated. His self-evident grief told its own story, a tragedy still fresh in the minds of the Stephen sisters and one that blighted their short stay in Cumbria.

The remainder of the week was carefully orchestrated with trips to Gretna Green, Carlisle and local beauty spots, most notably to the village of Gilsland to inspect a well-preserved section of Hadrian's Wall. A few years later and the excursion to Lanercost Priory in the Irthing valley, where generations of Howards lay buried, might have prompted an essay on the pleasures of romantic ruins but now Virginia's visit is recorded without elaboration. In this first year of her diary the entries following Stella's death in July had become noticeably shorter until by now they had dwindled to the briefest record of events. Her entry for Friday October 1st is typical: 'Watched Jack fishing. Went to Tuddenham. Took photos. Lord & Lady Morpeth to dinner. Rather awful.'[7] The following day signalled the end of her ordeal and she was, to her considerable relief, soon settled in the London train with Vanessa, steaming away from a country that, despite its name, had seemed not remotely like paradise.

Howard tombs, Lanercost Priory

Lanercost Priory

With an unnerving sense of completion Virginia's last journey north in June 1938 took her back to the borders, scene of that first disastrous holiday forty years earlier. The trip this time was altogether more successful, a leisurely touring holiday with Leonard prompted by memories of a visit on the eve of war in 1914, when the couple stayed at Wooler, and Virginia first fell in love with the Northumberland moors. Writing then to Ka Cox from The Cottage Hotel she had enthused:

> We have struck about the most beautiful country I've ever seen here. Except that it has no sea, I think it better than Cornwall – great moors, and flat meadows with very quick rivers. We are in an Inn full of north country people, who are very grim to look at, but so up to date that one blushes with shame. They discuss Thomson's poetry, and post impressionism, and have read everything, and at the same time control all the trade in Hides, and can sing comic songs and do music hall turns – in fact the Bloomsbury group was stunted in the chrysalis compared with them – [8]

Chollerford Bridge over the North Tyne

This time (1938) they took in Sir Walter Scott's shrine at Dryburgh Abbey, the Isle of Skye and Wordsworth's cottage on the return leg. Their itinerary included an overnight stop at The George in Piercebridge, built on the site of an important Roman station where Watling Street crossed the River Tees, and where they were joined for lunch by a large hunting party. The scene was replicated the following day at Chollerford in Northumberland, the point at which Hadrian's Wall traverses the North Tyne river. In another George Inn (England's patron saint was frequently invoked in this troubled outpost) with the 'bubbling and boiling'[9] river flowing beside its garden, the Woolfs witnessed another hunt that seemed to consist largely of elderly ladies 'in tweed suits with the pads of otters or foxes mounted in gold pinned to their breasts'[10]. Here, on the west bank beyond a five-arched bridge (1771) spanning the river, are the remains of *Cilurnum*, most beautifully situated of all the Roman forts and the only surviving cavalry station on the wall. One evening they walked two miles up this richly wooded stretch of the Tyne to Houghton Castle, a perfectly arranged tower house, one of many fortified houses in what was once bandit country, where even the rectories were embattled. On the eve of another war the place appeared altogether more civilised:

> ... oh me! the river running and the old Castle, and the grass path and the people – peasants, wandering along the bank, and talking to us, like something in the time of Elizabeth, so that I felt I was actually in Shakespeare, one of the northern ones.[11]

Housesteads south granary

At Chollerford the Woolfs were only fifteen miles east of Gilsland where all those years before Virginia had been taken to see Hadrian's Wall for the first time. On this latest occasion the Woolfs motored the few miles to Housesteads, the largest and most thoroughly excavated fort on the wall that Virginia thought looked more like the foundations of a group of farm buildings. The wall itself she found more dramatic astride a switchback outcrop of craggy volcanic rock crowned with trees like 'a wave with a sharp crest, as of a wave drawn up to break.'[12] While Leonard cleaned the spark plugs Virginia sat reading Greek poetry in translation, gazing out across wild open moorland covered in purple heather with 'Sheep bedded in the long turf like pearls'[13], an immortal landscape unchanged since Hadrian built his wall:

Hadrian's Wall,
wood engraving,
C C Webb, c.1930

... the landscape that to me is the loveliest in the world; miles and miles of lavender coloured loneliness, with one thread white path ... the immensity and tragedy and the sense of the Romans, and time, and eternity; and then the wild white hawthorn, and the sheep cropping, and 3 little white headed boys playing in a Roman camp ... d'you know how suddenly a country expands an airball in ones mind – I mean states a mood completely that was existent but unexpressed, so that at every turn of the road, its like half remembering, and thinking it can't be coming, but then it does? – a feeling a dream gives? and also that it is oneself – the real Virginia or Ethel, the dormant, the eternal?[14]

This is an extract from a letter Virginia wrote a few days later (26th June, 1938) to Ethel Smyth in which she firmly states her intention to return to the wall 'if I live long enough.'[15] She never did – three years later she was dead.

III
THE FENS

A test of friends

At the beginning of August 1899 all four Stephen children found themselves standing on the platform of an isolated Fenland station awaiting the omnibus that would take them to the rectory at the far end of the village. They had come to this desolate spot some six miles north east of Huntingdon at the behest of cousin Dorothea Stephen, a frequent and unwelcome visitor to the family's London residence at Hyde Park Gate. Earlier that year she had written to Virginia and Vanessa: '"We shall be very glad if you will spend the summer near us at Warboys – only we think you will have to change the name to Peace Girls." !!!!'[1] The flurry of exclamation marks came later in a letter from Virginia to her cousin Emma Vaughan.

Arriving on a day overcast and wet, Virginia's initial response to this landscape of endless horizons was decidedly unenthusiastic: '... the country thro' which our train passed was dull in the extreme.'[2] Situated on a spur of higher ground thrust out into the heart of the fen, the village of Warboys appeared equally unattractive. Strung out along the main street this mixture of Victorian chapels, institute buildings and grey brick houses was a rather dreary product of the railway era, but just as Virginia's spirits began to flag the weather brightened dramatically:

> ... the sun shot a shaft of light down; & we beheld a glorious expanse of sky – this golden gauze streamer lit everything in its light; & far away over the flat fields a spire caught the beam & glittered like a gem in the darkness & wetness ...'[3]

Buoyed up by this dazzling spectacle on the short journey from the station, during which time they passed no less than nine public houses, Virginia felt moved to declare 'Room for Dorothea's band of Hope here!'[4] a sly reference to her evangelical cousin's membership of the London Temperance Society.

Warboys clock tower

The few buildings of any distinction lie at the far end of the street beyond that ubiquitous feature of Fenland villages, the Jubilee clock tower (1887). Here the stately parish church of St Mary Magdalen rises from the fields, its medieval broach spire a landmark for miles around. The 17th century manor house immediately north of the churchyard with its large shaped gables and red brickwork already laid in Flemish bond, is a clear reminder that it was Dutch engineers who first drained the Bedfordshire Levels. Opposite, and hidden from view by a generous belt of trees, stands the old rectory, now Moat House, the large gault brick residence that was to be home to the Stephen family for the next six weeks.

The manor house, Warboys

A few days later (7th Aug.) Virginia spent the morning drifting listlessly in a punt on the moat in 'this eternal throbbing heat'[5] unable to throw off the mood induced by the strange, flat country where '[s]uch melting gray of sky, land & water is the very spirit of monotony.'[6] A stroll in the churchyard seemed appropriate to her melancholy:

... full of sombre tombstones, with queer carvings & angels heads sprawling over date & name and all. There are many graves that are nameless; & I was startled to think that I was walking over some ancient dust forgotten & undistinguished from the hillocks of the field. The graves rise in swelling mounds side by side all along the bottom of the churchyard.[7]

St Mary Magdalen

Days later Virginia discovered for herself the architectural delights of St Mary Magdalen, most notably its impressive Norman chancel arch, its 13th century font with stiff-leaf decoration and its Perpendicular windows 'whose long brass latches are picturesque though doubtless inefficient'.[8] She was accompanied on this occasion by the curate in charge, 'the first live specimen I have ever shaken hands with ...'[9]. Although resident in the village for nearly a year, he knew surprisingly little about his church but at dinner that evening managed to redeem himself with amusing snippets of village gossip. Mr Blake Milward was by inclination High Anglican and seemed ill at ease among the predominantly Baptist population of Warboys who practiced total immersion every Easter in a pond near the station. The only things that made life tolerable in this isolated outpost were a healthy contempt for the rector's wife, a Mrs Proudie figure with whom he was in open hostility, and the opportunity to shoot rabbits. Acceptance into the community was for Virginia a remote possibility:

> The people about here are a peculiar race. So imbedded are they in their own delving pursuits, living lonely self contained lives, with a few strong religious opinions that only serve to narrow their minds, that a stranger is in their eyes a most contemptible creature.[10]

As the temperature soared Virginia and Adrian decided to postpone their daily exercise until after tea. With no 'disturbing Hills'[11] to slow their progress this was perfect cycling country and the two often rode for miles along narrow straight tracks beside the dykes in the cool of the evening. Surveying a landscape alive with the sound of harvest Virginia felt more kindly disposed to the Fens and its inhabitants. Having persevered with a rather scratchy pen her inability to describe the scene to her satisfaction was matched only by her wretched handwriting.

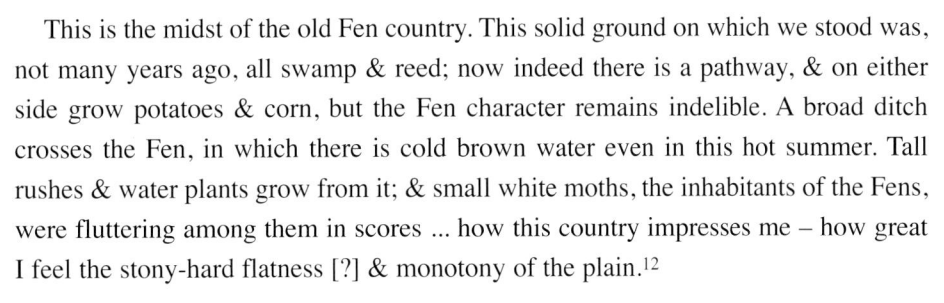

> This is the midst of the old Fen country. This solid ground on which we stood was, not many years ago, all swamp & reed; now indeed there is a pathway, & on either side grow potatoes & corn, but the Fen character remains indelible. A broad ditch crosses the Fen, in which there is cold brown water even in this hot summer. Tall rushes & water plants grow from it; & small white moths, the inhabitants of the Fens, were fluttering among them in scores ... how this country impresses me – how great I feel the stony-hard flatness [?] & monotony of the plain.[12]

Just four miles north of Warboys, stands the small market town of Ramsey where, a few days before, the train carrying the Stephen entourage had stopped briefly on its journey from London. Having consulted her guide book and discovered the ease with which she could traverse the countryside, Virginia decided it might be worth cycling the short distance in search of monastic remains. Situated on a low rise Ramsey Abbey had once been one of the great religious houses in the Fens to rival Crowland and Ely. This outpost of Christianity, surrounded by a huge expanse of 'dense & melancholy marshes'[13] teeming with fish and wild fowl, was well placed to nurture the contemplative life until, at the Dissolution, the great Benedictine church was pulled down and pillaged for its building materials. Some of the

The c13 font
St Mary Magdalen

more ornate pieces of Barnack stone were used as garden sculpture including the section of elaborately moulded column from the nave arcade that found its way to Warboys rectory. Here, beneath a large chestnut tree, it is still used as a chopping block.

The chopping block, Warboys old rectory

The gatehouse, Ramsey Abbey

Today Ramsey is an unremarkable place, redeemed at the far end of the High Street by an attractive group of buildings arranged around a spacious green. Here the series of pretty estate cottages is offset on one side by the parish church and opposite by a richly ornamented fragment of the Abbey gatehouse, inside which is the marble effigy (c.1230) of Aelwin, founder of the Abbey in 969. Ramsey appears to have left little impression on its young visitor who copied out the bare historical facts from the relevant volume of Kelly's 1885 Directory without further comment, but years later when casting around for ideas it may have provided Virginia with a name for the Ramsay family in *To The Lighthouse*.

The stone bridge and medieval chapel, St Ives

The town of St Ives, unlike its Cornish namesake, receives only a passing reference in Virginia's journal. In her entry for August 18th, 1899, entitled 'Warboys Distractions', the stone bridge with its medieval chapel built by the Abbots of Ramsey warrants a mention and by the end of the day there are additional notes on the town's history. The weekly market granted a charter by Edward I, the disastrous fire of 1680 and St Ives' most famous resident, Oliver Cromwell, are all dutifully transcribed from Kelly's Directory in the manner of her Ramsey notes. The sudden interest in the town had been prompted by an unscheduled ride through its cobble streets on her way to a 'terrible oppressive gathering of Stephens'[14] beside the river at Godmanchester. The outing, planned well in advance with the help of Bradshaw's Railway Guide, had begun ominously enough. Having almost missed the train at Warboys the Stephen family eased themselves with some relief into a third class carriage and gazed out of the window: 'All around were gray flat fields with rain swishing over them & the pollard trees sobbing in the wind.'[15]

The protracted journey involving several changes had terminated at St Ives station where, due to a misunderstanding over platforms, they had missed their connection to Huntingdon and were being driven through a succession of picturesque villages in a hastily arranged pony trap – 'such antiquity grows depressing after a time'[16] – to a belated luncheon with a daunting collection of relatives who 'bring with them the atmosphere of the lecture room; they are severe, caustic & absolutely independent & immoveable [sic]'[17]. The company and the weather conspired to produce what Virginia concluded was a 'somewhat grim day of pleasure'[18]. A boat trip was followed by a dreary walk along the river bank before the guests eventually decided on a place to spread their picnic:

Picture us uncomfortably seated on a towing path; half the party in a ditch, the other half in long grass – a cold wind blowing, with occasional drops of rain – no glow in east or west – but a grey melancholy vista of sky. Sir Herbert fought wasps & eat bread & jam – then we slowly packed our basket & started back for Godmanchester. I sat in one boat with Lady Stephen ... The rain fell now with a vengeance.[19]

Houghton vernacular

There can be little doubt that the Stephen children were relieved to return to the comfort and seclusion of Warboys where they could resume their passion for bugging. The first stage of their sugar campaign, described in great detail by Virginia, involved smearing a selection of trees in the grounds with a lethal mixture of rum and thick black treacle. Later that evening, under cover of darkness, the intrepid explorers set about their deadly business.

Julian, dressed like a brigand and clutching his jar of poison, was followed by Vanessa in evening dress and shawl carrying a net, Virginia holding a bicycle lamp 'of brilliant but uncertain powers of illumination'[20] and Adrian, 'a supernumerary amateur of no calling ... proficient in the art of obscuring the lamp at critical moments.'[21] Gurth, the family pet, who proved adept at catching moths 'for no entomological purpose whatever'[22], completed the expedition. At each tree the more interesting specimens, already intoxicated by the sticky liquor, were swiftly despatched by the leader with a single drop from his uncorked bottle. As the lantern bearer argued in her own defence: 'Death might come more painfully.'[23]

For Virginia the best form of relaxation available at Warboys was to lie in the punt with a good selection of reading material. Here, drifting through the duck weed, she developed the idea for an outrageous piece of spoof journalism written for the amusement of her cousin Emma Vaughan, in which the author is sent by a local paper as its special correspondent to report a fatal accident at Warboys rectory. The article that appeared in the Huntingdonshire Gazette beneath the headline 'TERRIBLE TRAGEDY IN A DUCK POND' recounts the harrowing tale of three young people drowned when their punt capsized during a moonlight excursion on the lake. Written in a style more suitable to a Victorian melodrama a few days after her 'grim day of pleasure'[24], Virginia showed commendable restraint when she might well have felt like choosing relatives other than Emma and Adrian to accompany her to a watery grave:

> The angry waters of the duck pond rose in their wrath to swallow their prey – & the green caverns of the depths opened – & closed – The cold moonlight silvered the path to death – & perhaps tinged the last thoughts of the unfortunate sufferers with something of its own majestic serenity. We know not if their end was promptly consummated, or if terrible shrieks & agonized struggles for air preceded the merciful rest that soon was theirs. Alone, untended, unsoothed, with no spectator but the silver moon, with no eye to weep, no hand to caress, three young souls were whelmed by the waters of the duck Pond.[25]

Throughout her Warboys Journal, Virginia's frequent use of the word 'melancholy' to describe the Fens and her interest in the many unmarked graves beyond the rectory gates suggest an unhealthy affinity with this strange, watery landscape. Despite its self-mocking tone her 'duck pond tragedy' – death by drowning – foretells her own suicide years later in the Sussex Ouse

Warboys old rectory. The moat, with remains of its landing stage, was the setting for Virginia's 'Terrible Tragedy in a Duck Pond'

with unnerving accuracy. Virginia's dream of a Fenland funeral procession is in stark contrast to this light-hearted exercise in tabloid journalism. The traders' carts full of mourners creep like huge black beetles along a bone white track that stretches away to the far horizon. These people, who in their poverty and their grief are inescapably bound to the black fen and utterly exposed to the elements, resemble characters from one of Hardy's tragic novels, but as the funeral passes by so the image takes on a more sinister tone.

They came from the east along the absolutely straight white road. We saw them crawling towards us with the sky heaping clouds & the wind blowing blue spaces around them. As we passed them, a boy looked down at us very sullenly & with the peculiar sodden depressed look that Fen men & women have; they were absolutely silent; & the procession went on to the heart of the Fen. I dreamt most vividly of this last night; how I looked into the womens faces; & the carts passed on and into the [night?] they were going back to some strange dark land, & they said the only time they saw the light of day was when they came to Warboys to bury their dead.[26]

As she became more familiar with the surrounding countryside its distinctive ethereal appeal soon dispelled any reservations Virginia still had for the Fens: 'There is a curious feeling in this land of infinite sky: so that you can become a weather prophet lying on yr. back.'[27] By September 3rd the whole of her entry for that day is devoted to a description of the most glorious Turneresque sunset, but after just a few days at Warboys she is already celebrating her new found enthusiasm for the great cloudscapes and wide horizons. Cycling back from Huntingdon with a string bag of melons bumping against her knees, Virginia was in rapturous mood; a mood conveyed to Emma Vaughan the following day.

You dont see the sky until you live here. We have ceased to be dwellers on the earth. We are really made of clouds. We are mystical and dreamy and perform Fugues on the Harmonium ... I shall think it a test of friends for the future whether they can appreciate the Fen country. I want to read books about it, and to write sonnets about it all day long. It is the only place for rest of mind and body, and for contentment and creamy potatoes and all the joys of life. I am growing like a meditative Alderney cow. And there are people who think it dull and uninteresting!!!![28]

Virginia was alert to the most subtle change of atmosphere and on her last day at Warboys (20th September), her mood of melancholy had acquired a distinctly autumnal flavour: 'a sharp wind comes racing over the plain, and brown coveys of partridges rise from the stubble ...'[29] The hedges were now laden with berries, the colours more subdued, but the most distinctive sign was always a 'mellow clearness in the air'[30] that brought with it '... odours of burning wood & weeds; and delicious moisture from the shaven earth; it is cleaner & more virile; it is autumn in its youth, before decayed woods &

ENGLISH HOURS

Cloudscape over the Fens

weeping vapours have come to end its substance.'[31] The sight of weeds burning on a hill when they had last cycled to Ramsey seemed to epitomise the changing season and by way of illustration she refers her reader to Millais' picture 'Autumn Leaves'.

Later that year Thoby went up to Trinity and Virginia soon came to know his close undergraduate circle, but whether Lytton Strachey, Saxon Sydney-Turner or the rest were ever dragged out into the Fens and subjected to her test of friendship remains uncertain. What *is* clear is that Virginia enjoyed her holiday in the Fens more than any other apart from those in her beloved Cornwall. Evident too in her letter to Emma Vaughan is a precocious literary style which, according to Quentin Bell, with its 'pace, its mockery, its exaggeration, its flights of fancy'[32] came to characterise her more mature correspondence. Here and in her Warboys Journal Virginia first discovered her unique literary talent.

IV
THE NEW FOREST

A little sleek and a little tame

For a time, following Leslie Stephen's decision to vacate Talland House, the New Forest had become the location of choice for the family's annual holiday. In 1898 they were at Ringwood Manor, a lovely early c18 house with stables that Virginia considered comfortable but, to her eyes, not attractive. But then the summer was unbearably hot, tempers became frayed and there had been the usual procession of unwelcome guests – no holiday was complete without a visitation from the Fisher cousins. Between 1900 and 1902 the Stephens were at Fritham House in the village of Bramshaw near the Wiltshire border. To judge from the few surviving letters to Emma Vaughan and Violet Dickinson, Virginia spent much of the time on long solitary drives through the Forest in a pony and trap or riding along dusty tracks over the heath on her bicycle with Vanessa. It was here that she first met Thoby's Cambridge friend Lytton Strachey whose family had taken Cuffnells in the Forest, a rather grand house with sweeping views of the Isle of Wight.

The following summer (of 1903) the Stephen sisters were just over the border in Wiltshire staying at Netherhampton House (see Chapt.V). Here they visited the county's most famous tourist attractions; Stonehenge (twice), Wilton House and Salisbury Cathedral. When Virginia recorded, with some relief, that the 'last of the sights within reach has been accomplished '[1], she had just returned from a trip to Romsey Abbey some twenty miles south east of Salisbury. From her reading of Wordsworth's 'Tintern Abbey' she had arrived expecting 'ivied arches & mossy pillars standing un-roofed in the open air, like the ribs of a wrecked ship'.[2] Instead she found a small town on the banks of the Test gathered about its great abbey church and a statue of Lord Palmerston gazing out across the market place.

Virginia Stephen, 1902, George Beresford

Romsey Abbey, choir and south transept

The Benedictine foundation had been rebuilt on a grand scale by Henry de Blois, Bishop of Winchester, in the 12th century on the site of the original Saxon nunnery. The limestone had come from the same south Wiltshire quarries at Chilmark that had supplied the stone for Salisbury Cathedral. At the Dissolution the monastic church had been sold to the town thus sparing it the fate that befell the remaining conventual buildings, pillaged for their building materials. Virginia was at least spared the lifeless ruins that greeted her on a trip to Glastonbury Abbey some years later (see Chapt. IX).

The squat, rather inelegent outline of Romsey Abbey belies its magnificent interior, the most complete Norman church of any size in England, but its soaring nave arcades failed to impress the young visitor who, having reconciled herself to a dearth of romantic ruins, took a more critical view of the interior. The building, she decided, was stylistically confusing and a curious mixture of clear, secular light, clinical restoration – 'restorers too have laid their cloven hoof upon it'[3] – and architectural salvage. Carved fragments piled up in the side aisles looked more like 'a rubbish heap of Saints heads, & pious stone'.[4]

The Saxon crypt and 'rubbish heap of ... pious stone'

When Virginia returned to the Forest in 1904 to celebrate Christmas and the New Year with her sister and brothers they stayed on this occasion at Lane End, a newly built house made available by Sarah Duckworth (Aunt Minna) just outside Lyndhurst. Here she soon fell into the familiar daily rhythm: 'Read, wrote, cursed, & walked – all as usual'[5] and was soon writing effusively to Lady Robert Cecil:

It is the loveliest place ... We have Beech trees practically poking their heads in at the front door ... and Thoby saw a cow chasing a Fox in a field last night in the moonlight.[6]

THE NEW FOREST

At Violet Dickinson's suggestion Virginia had already begun submitting articles to Margaret Lyttelton, editor of the Women's Supplement of the *Guardian*. Encouraged by the publication of her first essay on the Brontës at Haworth (see Chapt.VI) she appeared at Lane End out of the London fog with an armful of books intent on developing her initial success as a feature writer: 'reading makes me intensely happy, and culminates in a fit of writing always.'[7] She took great care over an essay on the Forest in winter that has since been lost but to judge from her diary which she was now in the habit of using to rough out short, descriptive pieces, the finished article may have proved too florid in style for publication:

> The sunset makes all the air as though of melted amethyst; yellow flakes dissolve from the solid body of amethyst which is the west. Against this, standing as though in an ocean of fine air, the bare trees are deep black lines, as though drawn in Indian ink which has dried dull & indelible. The small branches & twigs make a fringe of infinitely delicate lines, each one distinctly cut against the sky. The highest tips of the branches are russet, & so is the top of the trunk, in the red sun light. ...[8] [etc].

Gnarled beech trees, the New Forest

She managed to avoid the pitfalls of 'nature notes' in the future. With the memory of Romsey Abbey still fresh in her mind she boarded a train for Christchurch on the edge of the Forest where the Priory church from which the town takes its name, was to be the subject of her next journalistic essay, published in the *Guardian* in July of that year. From the north, Christchurch is clearly visible across a large expanse of river meadows 'like a ship riding out to sea.'[9] Here the waters of the Avon and Stour 'loop and cross and entangle themselves like a silver chain'[10] before flowing out between mud flats into Chichester harbour. From the station Virginia made her way up the High Street towards the object of her visit: 'Christchurch resolves itself into one long street, which ... bursts at the top into its flower, which is the Priory Church.'[11]

Christchurch Priory and north transept turret

The crucial events in the history of Christchurch Priory bear a striking resemblance to those of Romsey Abbey. The first Saxon minster was replaced in 1150 by Ranulph Flambard's Augustinian Priory, an ambitious scheme of reconstruction continued by Henry I's cousin Richard de Redvers and spread over the next 100 years. Unlike its domestic buildings the present structure, a memorable conjunction of late Norman nave and Perpendicular chancel, survived the Dissolution to become the parish church. Virginia acknowledges its many and beautiful possessions without specific reference to either the north transept turret, a showpiece of Norman decoration, or the magnificent medieval reredos. She is duly impressed by the sharp detail of the stone work, presumably an allusion to the Priory's chief glory, the delicately carved Salisbury chantry, but this diary entry is no exercise in architectural history or the aesthetics of medieval craftsmanship. Having paid her respects Virginia is soon climbing the tower. Once out 'on the leads, with the sharp spine of the church running out beneath'[12] and encircled by water both fresh and salt, she declares the view to be the Priory's most memorable asset; only 'a breadth of flats, dun-coloured with feathery bulrushes, separat[ing] the land from the water.'[13]

Lane End, a plaque records Virginia's holidays 1904-06

Two years later Virginia was back in the Forest for Christmas at Lane End with only Adrian for company. She missed the hilarity of the Stephens' last Christmas there together and had by now grown tired of the Forest; this was to be her last holiday in Hampshire. Her feelings for the place on this occasion may have been coloured by the recent traumatic death from typhoid of Thoby (on 20th November 1906) and the impending loss of Vanessa to married life (she was in Wiltshire with Clive Bell at the home of his parents). The more immediate death of Fred Maitland, historian, author of *Life and Letters of Leslie Stephen* and a close family friend was yet another blow. He had been one of the few links with the past she had welcomed and her response to his death – '... the earth seems swept very bare'[14] – was reflected all around her in the ground hard with frost, the house difficult to keep warm and the silence broken only by the occasional deer and forest pony in search of food. The place was, she acknowledged, perfect for Christmas: 'You can almost fancy that the woods have been arranged for the festival, & hung with holly, & sprinkled with snow.'[15] But this traditional Dickensian picture and her awareness of the Forest as an artificial, preserved landscape ideal for the retired and the conservative, fuelled her growing dissatisfaction.

For why does the forest always disappoint me? & why does Christmas disappoint me too? . . . The forest is too benign and complaisant; it gives you all that you can ask; but it hints at no more. . . . To be candid the forest is a little sleek & a little tame; it is Saxon without any Celtic mysticism; it is flaxen and florid, stately & ornamental. We have no use for forests now, & yet this one is preserved reverently, when the old spirit has died out of it ... You will not find the real country man or woman here, anymore than you will find arduous fields that are still turned assiduously. No; the country labourers are wont to pose as characters learned in forest lore; ...[16]

Today the Forest is even more rigorously preserved as a Forest Park with all the paraphernalia of outdoor recreation. Having recently lost its original purpose as a forest through which the deer and fox have been hunted since the Conquest, it is now a benign playground for the nation's town dwellers with a network of picnic sites, caravan parks and visitor centres arranged beneath its spreading canopy. Out of season the Forest still manages to appear much as Virginia came to dislike it; governed by its Lord Warden, its verderers' courts and all its archaic customs so jealously guarded. No wonder she longed for: '... the dusky roll of some Northern moor, or the melancholy cliffs of Cornwall. ...'[17] where she could hear the wind and roar of the ocean.

V

WILTSHIRE

This is the bare bones of the earth

In August 1903 Virginia and Vanessa arrived in Wiltshire with a sick father and a nurse, bound for Netherhampton House just west of Salisbury. Leslie Stephen was dying of cancer and for Virginia in particular, who had lately grown much closer to her father, this last holiday together was both precious and poignant. It was also at times exacting, the stress alleviated by short excursions to stroll in the grounds of Wilton House or visit the nearby grave of the c17 poet and divine, George Herbert, in Bemerton church. Virginia's few surviving letters – to her closest confidantes Violet Dickinson and Emma Vaughan – chart her father's decline and 'a plague of males'[1] that descended on Netherhampton. They included various Fisher cousins whose parents, having decided their proximity was required, had rented a house in Salisbury's Close for the summer. The presence of Fishers who, Virginia was convinced, 'would have made Eden un-inhabitable'[2], could not entirely be ignored and the Stephen sisters were eventually obliged to spend 'a most depressing interview'[3] in the shadow of the cathedral.

Netherhampton House is hidden away in the Nadder valley behind a row of pleached limes and elaborate wrought iron gates surmounted by a coat of arms. Virginia took to it immediately: '... with a certain quaint dignity of its own, greatly mellowed by time. These little gray old houses are common all over England, but I doubt whether you find them elsewhere –'[4]. It was now rented to the sculptor Henry Furze and his family who had decorated it sympathetically, furnished it sparingly and were people of taste, Virginia's term of approval. She took up residence in a large, whitewashed attic, the same space later allocated to Walter de la Mare when a guest of the poet Henry Newbolt in the 1920s, and enjoyed views out across the fields to the bare outline of the downs. From a slender, columned porch at the side of the house visitors stepped out onto a wide grass walkway that led past herbaceous borders to a walled kitchen garden crammed with fruit and vegetables. This older rear wing of warm Tudor brick is all that survives of the original dower house, built by the Pembrokes of Wilton, where a succession of aged aunts had lived out their days. The distinction of Netherhampton House comes not from these domestic arrangements but the 'solemnly ashlar-faced'[4A] façade added in the early 18th century that delighted the young guest:

> ... a little gray stone house, too humble to be itself ornate, but evidently dating from an ornate period – & in its humble way an imitation of a genuine great house. There is some kind of architectural device of urns at intervals on the gables; there is a hollowed recess in the wall, meant perhaps, were the thing on a larger scale, to stand a statue in.[5]

Netherhampton House

Throughout her life Virginia was able to cope more effectively with a series of personal tragedies, in this instance the impending death of her father, by the very act of writing. For an account of her stay in Wiltshire readers must turn to the journal she resumed with renewed enthusiasm for the first time since her Warboys adventure and her subsequent breakdown. It takes the form of a series of brief, descriptive essays; a record of attractions visited and countryside explored that, by giving shape to her new surroundings, brought a measure of calm to her inner world. This search for order and meaning was, in some small measure, put to the test soon after her arrival when, standing on the croquet lawn, Virginia and Vanessa decided to walk over to Bemerton church, clearly visible across the water meadows. What promised to be a gentle stroll soon became a tortuous and hazardous undertaking. After a number of false starts that obliged them to scramble through hedges and under fences they became bogged down and only by removing their shoes and wading through a series of wide, shallow ditches did they eventually emerge onto a road, to the amusement of two farm labourers in the next field. Exhausted by their abortive efforts and now the subject of rustic humour, they returned home where, on consulting *Radcliffe's Official Guide*, Virginia came across a detailed explanation for the bewildering system of drainage channels that had thwarted their attempts to reach George Herbert's church.

Bemerton church

The water meadows of the Nadder valley and those of the other chalk rivers that converge on Salisbury like the fingers of an outstretched hand had, since the 17th century, been transformed by an intricate irrigation system. This ingenious form of land management played a vital part in the local economy. It was controlled by a sequence of wooden hatches which in spring were raised to divert river water and flood, or float, the adjoining meadows thereby increasing significantly the hay crop each year. Each landowner employed a 'drowner' to operate and maintain the system and his role in the agricultural year became as important as that of the solitary shepherd on the surrounding hills. Virginia had inadvertently stumbled upon a traditional farming practice that, by quoting Radcliffe, enabled her to translate the confusion of their riverine foray into a way of reading the peculiar subtleties of the valley landscape.

On the Edge of the Plain,
John Nash

Apart from occasional cycle rides on the hills above Brighton this holiday was Virginia's first real introduction to the sweeping chalk landscape peculiar to southern England that she came to know intimately in the shape of the Sussex downs. Here in Wiltshire on an evening drive to Broad Chalke and spurred on by Adrian's loud indifference to the scene she observed that: 'the sky above the chalkland is of a peculiar pale blue – as though something of the whiteness of the chalk were reflected in it.'[6] Lulled by its rhythmic undulations her response to this new landscape was both immediate and lasting:

As we drove along through lanes deeply cut in the chalk, I kept likening the downs to the long curved waves of the sea. It is as though the land here, all molten once, &

rolling in vast billows had solidified while the waves were still swollen & on the point of breaking. From a height it looks as though the whole land were flowing ... The villages have all sunk into the hollows between the waves; and the result is a peculiar smoothness & bareness of outline. This is the bare bones of the earth –[7].

As the summer wore on Virginia slipped effortlessly into the routine of country life at Netherhampton enlivened by the kind of long solitary walks on the hills that were to become such a regular feature of her time at Asheham and Rodmell. Here in Wiltshire, sounding more like the county's own nature mystic Richard Jefferies, she declared her love for the downs:

If I lived here much longer I should get to understand the wonderful rise & swell & fall of the land. It is like some vast living thing, & all its insects and animals, save man, are exquisitely in time with it. If you lie on the earth somewhere you hear a sound like a vast breath, as though it were the very inspiration of earth herself, & all the living things on her.[8]

The chalk hills were even then becoming Virginia's spiritual heartland but she always reserved a more critical eye for the works of man, in this instance the Earls of Pembroke in whose property the Stephens were staying. Wilton House had been the family seat of the Herberts for the last 350 years and Virginia felt obliged to visit the ancestral pile. Having trudged for a couple of

Wilton House, triumphal arch

miles beside a high brick wall and negotiated an oversize military statue of the 13th Earl positioned before the gates, the initial signs were not encouraging. Virginia made her entrance via the triumphal arch surmounted by an equestrian statue of Marcus Aurelius that had been brought down from its elevated position in the park to impress the visitors and remind the locals that 'the feudal spirit in England is not yet dead.'[9]

Wilton, it must be said, is one of the country's great stately houses although nothing survives of the original Elizabethan mansion except Holbein's porch, now an elegant if somewhat unlikely garden feature. The life of this building would have appealed to Virginia; a centre of artistic and scholarly excellence, presided over by the second countess, where Ben Jonson, Spenser, Marlowe and other luminaries of the day gathered including, most probably, Shakespeare. But the house that greeted Virginia was more a monument to the Pembroke dynasty, a mixture of lavish state rooms by Inigo Jones culminating in the Double Cube room designed to display Vandyke's celebrated family portraits. This was her first stately home and, having dutifully bought a ticket she joined several American ladies already assigned to a familiar type of rather frightful housekeeper:

William Herbert, 1st Earl of Pembroke by Hans Eworth

Wilton House

... willing to gratify our awed curiosity as to the Herbert family & their belongings – & at the same time she clearly felt herself to be socially our superior. She did the honours with the condescending air of one to whom Greek statues & Vandykes are a matter of course, but she expected our plebian respect. So we trooped behind her obediently & were submissively awe-struck.[10]

The house, with its stylistic confusion of antique furniture, architectural ornament and, despite the Vandykes, 'a still greater number of worthless'[11] pictures, was a disappointment. Knowing that her one shilling entrance fee would go towards the upkeep of Magdalen Hospital, a row of cottages built in 1832 by the Dowager Countess of Pembroke for a selection of aged servants, merely compounded Virginia's impression that the hand of privilege and deference extended to all aspects of life in the town.

... it is more smug & well pleased with itself than the majority of English villages ... that sit in the shadow of a great house ... Its whole world is circled by the 'Park'; its interest is concerned entirely with 'Her Ladyship' & the goings on at the Castle. In almost every street you can trace the influence of the Herbert family. The three inns of course are loyally christened after the various titles of the Pembrokes; their arms, slightly battered by weather hang from all the sign posts: they, in their turn have [ ] scattered fountains & almshouses all round them, & generally keep the village so tidy and sweet that it makes the most respectable setting for Wilton itself.[12]

Remains of St John's hospital encased in later almshouses

Historically the town had good reason to feel smug; it is one of the oldest boroughs in Wiltshire, once the county town, and a medieval centre of some importance with several large religious foundations including a famous

Benedictine nunnery replaced by Wilton House after the Dissolution. It could also boast twelve churches in Leyland's time, of which only the chancel of St Mary's survives in the Market Place. Wilton's most impressive church is its most recent, an Italianate Romanesque extravaganza by TH Wyatt built in 1843 and full of mosaics, barley twist columns, coloured marbles and a kaleidoscope of medieval glass; another monument to the Herbert family – sumptuous and indigestible. Today the Pembroke Arms opposite the triumphal arch is the only inn to bear the family crest and elsewhere the town appears to have shrugged off the more obvious signs of patronage as it sinks slowly beneath a relentless stream of vehicles, many in summer on their way to one of Wiltshire's great tourist attractions – Wilton House.

The great house was a salutary lesson and in later years Virginia only ever visited such places by invitation; Knole in the company of Vita Sackville-West and Garsington Manor as the guest of Ottoline Morrell. No holiday in Wiltshire is, however, complete without excursions to its most revered architectural monuments. Separated by just a few miles but several thousand years of history Stonehenge and Salisbury inevitably invite comparisons as shrines to two very different gods. The arrival of an enthusiastic young guest, one RC Norman who went on to become chairman of the BBC, provided the excuse for a site-seeing tour. Virginia noted that 'Providence has sent a very energetic visitor'[13] and they set out for Stonehenge on a beautiful summer's day. Following the sinuous course of the Avon out of Salisbury below Old Sarum they passed through some of the loveliest villages in Wiltshire; a string of thatched cottages and stone farmhouses each with 'its tiny roots deep twisted in to the main root of the land'[14], on through the Woodfords – Lower, Middle and Upper – until, beyond Durnford they emerged on to the Plain. Here they were greeted by a vast ancient landscape littered with Celtic field systems and Bronze Age barrows. There in the distance the unmistakable outline of the henge appeared far more compact than Virginia had imagined.

As a literary pilgrim Virginia had chosen her reading material with some care. Boswell's Hebridian journey was followed by *Tess of the d'Urbervilles* where, in Hardy's 'Temple of the Winds', the sun's first rays light up the figure of his 'pure woman' asleep on the sacrificial stone. Francis Kilvert had paid his own homage on a visit in 1875, approaching the stones on foot across a plain that 'heaved mournfully with great and solemn barrows.'[15] For Kilvert this temple to the old gods; 'The Enchanted Giants, the Silent Preachers, the Sleepless Watchers, the Great Cathedral on the Plain'[16], remained an

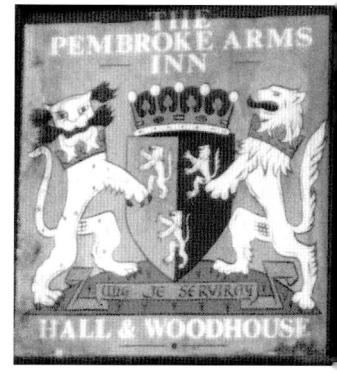

The Pembroke Arms sign

WILTSHIRE

awesome spectacle and the young curate instinctively removed his hat on entering the circle. Henry James concluded his own tour of Wessex three years earlier with a visit to Wiltshire. He was a writer whose style Virginia admired – she had with her a copy of *Roderick Hudson* and it may have brought to mind his Stonehenge essay first published in *Portraits of Places* (1883) in which:

Stonehenge

... It stands as lonely in history as it does on the great plain whose many-tinted green waves, as they roll away from it, seem to symbolise the ebb of the long centuries which have left it so portentously unexplained.[17]

Certainly Virginia's meditation, expressed more succinctly, shared his own sentiment on the enigma of the circle:

The singular, & intoxicating charm ... is that no one in the world can tell you anything about it ...

I felt as though I had run against the stark remains of an age I cannot otherwise conceive; [ ] a piece of wreckage washed up from Oblivion.[18]

The expedition proved so successful that the Stephens returned several days later, this time taking the high road out of Salisbury. The party put up at a farmhouse where they had 'the rare experience of managing entirely for [themselves]'[19] before walking across to picnic in the circle the following day surrounded by grazing sheep. Apart from the rather incongruous sight of a solitary policeman keeping watch over the stones they had the place and seemingly the 'whole ocean of plain'[20] entirely to themselves; a far cry from the perimeter wire, huge car park and approach tunnel that greet today's tourists.

Salisbury cathedral beside the Avon

As the summer holiday drew to a close Virginia occasionally found the 'age and deep repose'[21] of Netherhampton House a little stifling and took to the dusty lanes in search of some interesting diversion. Inevitably she was drawn, like so many travellers, by the spire of Salisbury's cathedral. Situated near the confluence of five rivers, the city appears to nestle in the palm of a gigantic, outstretched hand with its spire rising gracefully some 400 feet above the water meadows. This enduring symbol of Christianity has called the faithful for the last 750 years and today visitors arriving by train still peer out hoping to catch a glimpse of the landmark that will announce their destination. From the surrounding hills it acts like a magnet and on her walks Virginia found her 'eye wandering over the landscape'[22] in search of it. Approaching the spire along the river bank she found the stonework was always changing colour from bone white in brilliant sunshine to dark grey on a drab, overcast day. On reaching the Close she felt as though she were entering a world of 'ancient loveliness & peace.'[23]

– with the air of a very comfortably cushioned Sanctuary from the sins & weariness of the outer world. The old ladies who let their dresses sweep its turf are infected by the atmosphere; they move with extreme leisure & dignity – as though earthly affairs had no longer any power to hurry them. Yet I can well imagine that their precincts cover as much scandal of an innocent sort as any similar space in Mayfair or Belgravia.[24]

Arranged around the perimeter is a handsome and harmonious collection of Georgian town houses that stand guard over the sacred turf ensuring that 'nothing vulgar shall taint the air of the cathedral; they treasure up & absorb the precious incense it gives out.'[25] The visit to a Miss Fawcett, the kind of 'benevolent & mildly garrulous old lady'[26] who inhabits the outskirts of the Close, confirmed Virginia's worst fears:

So much ancient stone however fairly piled, & however rich with the bodies of Saints & famous men, seems to suck the vitality of its humble neighbours. It is like a great forest oak; nothing can grow healthily beneath its shade.[27]

By now her enthusiasm had begun to flag and she would have gladly exchanged this most precious and lifeless shrine for a bare hilltop. There she could be alone with her thoughts unfettered by a surfeit of history and reverence and comforted perhaps by the knowledge that in her solitude she too had become part of the Romantic tradition. Remote hills had always been realms of the imagination free from the constraints of the world below. Wordsworth came most readily to her mind but here in Wiltshire a band of more contemporary companions tramped these same ridgeway tracks. For Richard Jefferies the hill forts at Barbury and Liddington on the Marlborough Downs became charged with a mystical energy. Among his disciples the

Mompesson House, Cathedral Close

Great War poet Charles Sorley roamed over those same rampart hills 'where the old battered signpost stands.' In 1917 while stationed in the Wylye valley on the eve of his return to the front Jefferies' biographer, the poet Edward Thomas, took a last walk over the downs to lunch with the Newbolts in the very house where the Stephens were now staying.

Edward Thomas, linocut, Robin Guthrie

Sarsen stones, Fyfield Down, near Lockeridge

Virginia was first in the heart of this ancient barrow-strewn country with Leonard in December 1914, staying at Lytton Strachey's cottage in the village of Lockeridge just west of Marlborough. From here she declared: 'It is evidently magnificent country – to my thinking better – at least more solid – than Sussex – but L. don't agree.'[28] Memories of this same stretch of country surfaced years later when, touring the West Country with Leonard in 1930, Virginia wrote to Ethel Smyth: 'But Lord what a lovely country this is – England, I mean, and ever so much older than I thought. I want to live on Marlborough Down, most.'[29]

On a more prosaic level Virginia admired the dignified figure of the Wiltshire shepherd drifting with his flock across the plain or stretched out on the ground wrapped in a long black coat and surrounded by grazing sheep in a scene reminiscent of the Old Testament. For a week each September one of the greatest sheep fairs in southern England took place at Wilton. Huge flocks were gathered together on the hillsides above and all manner of countryfolk and itinerant traders descended on the town where Virginia had ample opportunity to observe her noble rustic at close quarters:

A downland shepherd

His face is not coarsened; & yet is not the face of a man who has mixed with his fellow men ... it has the freshness & simplicity of a childs. The eye is perfectly clear & shrewd; the face is tanned red & brown, & creased with a multitude of fine lines ... come there when the eyes are screwed to observe the weather, or the brow is puckered against the wind – & have nothing whatever to do with any mental perplexity. His best coat is a relic of a more festive age, [ ] & is a rich chestnut, or plum colour, grown mellow with years; he wears corduroy breeches, a large felt hat; & he grasps a staff in his hand high up near the top.[30]

In this passage Virginia anticipates the writing of WH Hudson whose *A Shepherd's Life* (1910) is based on the recollections of James and William Lawes from the Wiltshire/Hampshire border village of Martin, regulars at the Wilton fair for many years. Hudson too, who had been brought up on the South American pampas, was struck by the piercing gaze of the old shepherds that seemed to stare right through him as though focused on some distant point on the horizon.

In later life Virginia seldom visited Wiltshire again and when she did her visits were brief, peripheral and usually served some purpose. In the summer of 1924 the *ménage à trois* that was Lytton Strachey, Carrington and Ralph Partridge, decided to move from their damp idyll at Tidmarsh Mill on the river Pang to the more spacious accommodation of Ham Spray, a square Regency house with its own walled garden and avenue approach four miles south of Hungerford. It was the last house in Wiltshire with wonderful views across the fields to Inkpen Hill and the whole sweep of chalk scarp. Virginia and Leonard called in October of that year 'on a wet misty day, & saw what the view might be in the sun; a flat meadow with trees in groups like people talking leading to the downs'[31]. There were no further visits to 'the frail lovely house'[32] until, in January 1932, they received the news that Lytton was dying of cancer. With his death four days later and Carrington's suicide the landscape they both loved, now tinged with grief, appeared inviolate, more emblematic:

Lytton Strachey

The Downs from Ham Spray, Dora Carrington, 1929-30

WILTSHIRE

... & the trees grouped & the down rising & the path climbing the down: this I noted, with envy thinking of my dogs barking, my downs ruined, as we sat at tea. I long sometimes for this sealed up, silent, remote country: long for its little villages; its muddy roads, its distance from Brighton and Peacehaven.[33]

Ham Spray in summer,
Dora Carrington, 1929

Kelmscott Manor,
woodcut, William Morris,
1891, for *News from Nowhere*

In July 1935 Virginia honoured her agreement to deliver the opening address at the Roger Fry memorial exhibition in Bristol. Later that day on a hot summer evening the Woolfs arrived exhausted in Bradford-on-Avon where they put up at the Old Court Hotel, 'an ancient workhouse in the valley; with disordered garden, [and] a stream with rotting sacks of old clothes'[34]. Relieved to be on their way the following morning they took a leisurely route via Avebury to the upper Thames valley. Just over the border in

65

Gloucestershire they wandered beside the river at Lechlade, celebrated by Shelley's 'Stanzas in a Summer Evening Churchyard', and watched the moon rise 'like a rose petal'[35]. During the day they had motored the few miles to Fairford and 'found the Carnival braying outside the church with the painted windows'[36], a distraction altogether less noisy than Concorde taking off from RAF Fairford that more recently shattered the calm. Here England's most complete set of late medieval glass – in St Mary's church – has miraculously survived the sonic boom. From here they travelled the short distance downstream to Kelmscott Manor on the banks of the Thames, lovingly described by its most famous resident William Morris in his utopian manifesto *News from Nowhere* (1892). Life in the country was not to everyone's taste however; Rossetti compared the village to 'the doziest dump of old grey beehives' but Virginia enjoyed their briefest of visits:

> In this country everything is made of silver grey flaky stone, & the houses cluster round, with their little gables, all crowded, ancient, with roses, with haystacks, & the river flowing in the great grass meadows, all untouched, beyond the builders ring ... [37]

Kelmscott Manor is now in trust but was then still a private house and the Woolfs had to satisfy their curiosities with a peep over the wall before setting off home to Sussex.

VI

THE YORKSHIRE DALES

*Great melancholy moors, sweeping all round us,
like some tragic audience, mutely attendant*

Following her disastrous trip to Corby Castle in 1897 Virginia did not venture north again until the late summer of 1904, a more modest journey on this occasion but in circumstances not far removed from her Cumbrian excursion. The death of Leslie Stephen in February had plunged her into another prolonged bout of madness during which she first attempted suicide. By September she had recovered sufficiently to join the rest of the family on holiday at Teversal, an Elizabethan manor house remodelled a few years earlier in Neo-Jacobean style and just north of DH Lawrence's mining village of Eastwood. From her letters to Violet Dickinson she was clearly responding well to the daily routine of long walks followed by tennis and afternoon excursions to the great houses of Derbyshire – Haddon Hall and Hardwick Hall in the next parish. As the voices in her head receded she longed for a return to London and the new family house, 46 Gordon Square, where she could resume writing. Her convalescence gathered pace in Cambridge where she stayed for much of late October/early November with a Quaker aunt; wrote long, expansive letters to Violet Dickinson and, encouraged by her doctor, arranged to spend a week in the Yorkshire Dales with her cousin William Vaughan and his family.

Passengers on the Leeds to Kendal railway still gaze in mild disbelief as the name 'Giggleswick' comes into view. 'Why' people ask themselves 'does the place display such a childish sense of humour?' Is it some collective response to the proximity of Wigglesworth emanating from the dormitories of Giggleswick School or the guffaws that greet each reference to 'Old Father Tems,' the local name for the Tems Beck that runs through the village and into the Ribble? There is in truth nothing much to laugh about in Giggleswick but its place alongside Tarring Neville, Little Fryup and, of course, Shellow Bowells, in the pantheon of England's silliest place names, is assured. Not surprisingly the village has received its fair share of attention from humorists since it acquired its own Shakespeare festival in an episode of 'Hancock's Half Hour'. Its most famous resident, the broadcaster Russell Harty, who once taught at the school, had soon found that being gay in Giggleswick was no joke. His friend and fellow Yorkshireman, Alan Bennett, who plundered the school register for names that appear in *Forty Years On,* would also have been aware of Woolf's connection with the place. The play draws indirectly on her memoirs and ten years later Bennett's fascination with the novelist was acknowledged in the title of his television play *Me, I'm Afraid of Virginia Woolf.*

The chapel above Giggleswick School

William Vaughan had only just been appointed head of Giggleswick School, the first secular head in its long history, when Virginia arrived on the first of two visits during a cold snap in November 1904. Her appearance had been preceded by a letter from Vanessa advising the Vaughans that although her sister was restored to normal health she was still not sleeping well and should not be allowed too much exercise. Virginia found a group of buildings, 'grey and forbidding according to the Victorian ideals of scholastic architecture'[1], 'in a little hollow by itself, with great craggy moors on all four sides'[2]. The severity of the school was, and still is, softened by wooded grounds spread about the lower slopes overlooking the playing fields and the village gathered around St Alkelda's church. Once settled in the headmaster's house she was writing to Violet Dickinson:

> Here I am sitting at my window under the moors, which are all white with snow and frost, and the temperature is below freezing. I keep warm with a fire, and a fur rug; and I might be in the heart of the Alps ... The country with its moors breaking into gray stone and gray stone walls instead of hedges and stone houses reminds me of Cornwall, and I always expect to find the Atlantic.[3]

Headmaster's house, Giggleswick School

William Vaughan MA

The hills beckoned but Virginia found herself drawn reluctantly into the busy life of the school. William's wife, Madge, had become her great friend while staying with the Stephens in London following the death of her father and Virginia had not forgiven her cousin for removing such an attractive and talented companion to the wilds of Yorkshire. To begin with she seemed determined to find fault with William, an ambitious young man who eventually became headmaster of Rugby. She considered him thick-headed and 'conventional to the back bone'[4], a man who 'loves all the small dignities and duties of his position'[5] and who disapproved of the dragon tales with which she delighted his children. Madge however was 'like a starved bird'[6]; she longed for more stimulating company but found herself constantly thwarted by the obligations of her position. It comes as something of a surprise therefore to find that less than two weeks later Virginia felt more generously disposed towards the Vaughans. They were now a devoted couple:

'She worships him, and refers to him in everything; and there is a great deal that is charming and clever about him besides all his solid good qualities.'[7] By now her irritation had found a new focus:

> Oh Lord those bells! The Vicar seems determined that those who don't go to Church shall have their evening spoilt. It is deafening. I think the ringers are trying to keep themselves warm with hard arm-work.[8]

St Alkelda's, Giggleswick

The explanation for this change of heart is contained in her second letter to Violet Dickinson. She had by then been allowed out on the snow-clad moors alone and, more importantly, she had just completed her first article for the *Guardian*, not today's national broadsheet but an obscure weekly magazine for Anglo-Catholic clergymen. It was, however, a start and, significantly, she

THE YORKSHIRE DALES

chose as her subject the parsonage at Haworth, once home to the nation's most celebrated literary sisters. Armed with a copy of Elizabeth Gaskell's *Life of Charlotte Brontë* Virginia travelled with Madge through a wintry landscape like 'a vast wedding cake, of which the icing was slightly undulating; the earth was bridal in its virgin snow'[9]. They arrived on the branch line from Keighley to find that Milltown, 'dingy and commonplace'[10], bore little resemblance to the Haworth of Virginia's imagination. The stone terraces etched against the snow 'climb the moor step by step in little detached strips ... so that the town instead of making one compact blot on the landscape has contrived to get a whole stretch into its clutches'[11]. Dismayed by the prospect she wondered 'whether pilgrimages to shrines of famous men ought not to be condemned as sentimental journeys'.[12] Virginia proved to be an informed, if reluctant, guide whose sense of anticipation throughout her visit is tempered by her experience of the place.

Anne, Emily and Charlotte Brontë

Church and parsonage, Haworth, from Mrs Gaskell's *Life*

The Brontë museum at the top of the steep cobbled street had recently been opened above a branch of the Yorkshire Penny Bank (now the tourist information centre). It housed 'a pallid and inanimate collection of objects'[13] and as Virginia reflects on the transient personal relics that have outlived their young owners she grudgingly admits the wisdom of their preservation. She records too how the church had been almost entirely rebuilt by the Victorians except for the tower and pauses to read the memorial slab erected to members of the Brontë family before making her way across the remarkable collection of flat gravestones, 'a pavement lettered with dead names'[14], towards the object of her pilgrimage. There in the churchyard she notes with a mixture of pleasure and relief that the simple arrangement of church, school and parsonage still resembled the little print in Mrs Gaskell's *Life* (1857). Apart from the large gabled wing added in 1878, the front hedge and the clumps of sycamores planted by a later incumbent 'wishing a little space between life and death'[15], the plain Georgian rectory remained exactly as it had been in Charlotte's day. Built of millstone grit, the 'ugly yellow-brown stone'[16] quarried locally, was in appearance a little too severe for Virginia's taste. Having been shown inside she decided that Haworth parsonage was an altogether unremarkable shrine 'though tenanted by genius'[17] and that had she been the incumbent she 'should often feel inclined to exorcise the three famous ghosts'[18]. It was to be another twenty four years before the Brontë Society was able to acquire the building and relocate its collection of relics from premises in the High Street.

First home of the Brontë museum

Haworth churchyard

The excursion had given Virginia plenty of material and she returned to Giggleswick in buoyant mood, dashing off her article in less than two hours. She was clearly intrigued by the relationship between writers and the landscape and returned to the theme a few months later with reviews of 'Dickens Country' and 'Thackeray Country' in an article for the *Times Literary Supplement* (March 1905) entitled 'Literary Geography'. 'Wordsworth and the Lakes' appeared in the *TLS* in June the following year

Haworth rectory

just after the author's second visit to Giggleswick – Virginia returned to the Dales for two weeks in April 1906 accompanied by her dog Gurth and a large box of books. Determined to pursue a more independent existence on this occasion she decided to take lodgings in the village with a Mrs Turner. Once installed she declared 'I lead the life of a Solitary'[19] and soon fell into a simple daily routine of reading and writing interrupted by meals, a walk on the hills with Gurth and tea with Madge. With memories of Haworth revived by her return to Yorkshire she was soon writing with studied enthusiasm to Violet Dickinson:

There is a Greek austerity about my life which is beautiful and might go straight into a bas relief. You can imagine that I never wash, or do my hair; but stride with gigantic strides over the wild moorside, shouting odes of Pindar, as I leap from crag to crag, and exulting in the air which buffets me, and caresses me, like a stern but affectionate parent! This is Stephen Brontëised; almost as good as the real thing.[20]

This time Virginia's journal, silent throughout her first visit, is more instructive, especially in her response to this exhilarating landscape; bare limestone hills of sombre beauty that again reminded her of Cornwall: 'the moors rise in waves all round; great crags of rock make a back ground, dimly seen in the April twilight & wild scents of the moor are driven in at the open window.'[21] Giggleswick, she discovers, is an ideal base from which to explore, elevated by its surroundings to the status of 'a discreet little Northern town, swept clean & simplified, out of all pettiness & vulgarity by the nobility of the country in which it lies.'[22] Virginia's walks took her out in every direction. One route she christened the Sacred Way because 'it leads beneath such tremendous hills, pale with shivered sheets of stone'[23], but even in 1906 the lanes were clogged with cars and bicycles over the Easter weekend and she soon struck out over the hills.

Limestone outcrop on the Settle-Kendal road

The Yorkshire Dales are limestone country, not the golden stone that lights up the Cotswolds but the harder grey limestone of the Carboniferous. This austere landscape of sudden vertical rock faces, known locally as 'scars', is covered over its lower slopes with layers of loose stones that had Virginia clinging desperately to thorn bushes in an attempt to arrest her descent. Once safely at the bottom she declared that a walk in such terrain 'tends to be rather an heroic undertaking'[24]. Here mountain streams disappear mysteriously down fissures in the ground with names like Gaping Gill and Bogarts Roaring Hole only to bubble to the surface just as suddenly hundreds of feet below. Caves high up on the Fells had once been colonised by packs of hyenas before their occupation by early hunter-gatherers who left behind tools fashioned from reindeer antlers. Attermire Cave, one of a group above Settle, had been discovered in the mid-19th century and on Easter Sunday, driven out of the village by Giggleswick's brass band, Virginia decided to attempt the ascent of Attermire – as she described it – making it sound like a climb of Alpine proportions. There is no mention of any cave and the path proved steep and devious but she was finally rewarded by a wonderful view:

... a strange country. You get into a desolate sea of moors, gray as bone, with but a sprinkling of green on them. These merge into each other, sink & swell again, till one can reach no further. No road or house seems to adventure out there; & the likeness to a barren sea scape is unavoidable.[25]

To the south west of Giggleswick the moors are different again, their flanks smoother and well drained as they build like gathering clouds towards the rounded summits of Bowland Forest and Burn Moor. The lower slopes form a wide transitional belt grazed by sheep, rising from the valleys of the Ribble and Wenning. Here Virginia is again a keenly observant and accurate witness to the most subtle changes of topography as she walks in silence but for the mournful cry of curlews wheeling overhead:

You walk upon very gentle downs, which fold themselves into steep hollows, & are fringed with slender groves of trees. It is an undulating, & suave country, lacking the abrupt majesty of the moors, but excelling them in a certain charm; a kind of pathos from its more immediate connection with low human kind. One gray farm, with its walled garden, will do much to humanize a whole sweep of field and down ... for the land remains a half tame thing; with all & wild creatures fearing for freedom in its eyes.[26]

Dales landscape with field barns

Another walk in this 'by no means cheerful & domestic, but melancholy & appealing'[27] countryside took her across High Rigg behind Giggleswick School which, despite its name, fails to reach a modest one thousand feet. It does however form an important watershed with becks rushing away on either side and a platform from which the whole sweep of the land is clearly realised:

The moors rise & roll away, for miles on either side, tossing themselves into great promontories like Ingleborough, or in to strange sugar loaf blocks, & then surging on their way again till they reach the Lake [District].[28]

Lawkland Hall

From here Virginia dropped down into a lane running along a valley that took her past Lawkland Hall, an old stone manor house with a massive central tower and rows of mullion windows that had been home to the Ingleby family since 1572. Its position and general air of self sufficiency she found appealing. It was, she considered:

... too small to be restored, & thus a beautiful specimen of simple domestic building, standing just off the road where everyone may see it. All its graceful gables & worn traceries are there untouched; & it is flanked by rough farm houses, of an earlier date still perhaps.[29]

Vanessa arrived for the second week and the two set out for the hamlet of Feizor, just a mile of so from Lawkland with 'a wizard like name, to be set beside others like Attameier [sic], as something singular, & belonging to no regular system'[30]. Tucked into the base of a hill below Pot Scar, Feizor is at the end of a narrow lane off the Settle to Kendal road but the two sisters decided on a less orthodox approach through sheep-strewn hills in a 'strange vale...sequestered from wind or any blast from the outside world, a dreamlike hollow between gray moors'[31] until they eventually found themselves suspended above the huddle of farms and cottages. Before descending Virginia, contemplating the isolation with an urban mind, thought 'what an odd fate it was to live in an old stone house all the days of one's life in the village of Feizor when the whole of the world lies open to one.'[32] Leaving the place to its fate they walked on along the grassy track which connects it to the outside world, ignoring the demands of some roadside tinkers, before the weather closed in:

> The great melancholy moors, sweeping all round us, like some tragic audience, mutely attendant, grew black & veiled with mist. Rain came down & the country seemed well pleased at this change of mood. Storm & rough weather suit it better than bland & innocent skies. But words! words! You will find nothing to match the picture.[33]

Feizor

Virginia returned to the Dales only once and then in rather odd circumstances but from her journal it is clear she again revelled in the freedom of the hills and all the subtle changes of atmosphere and topography she had experienced on her Giggleswick walks. In the early hours of June 29th 1927 she and Leonard boarded a packed train with Vanessa's son Quentin and the

Nicolsons, (Harold and Vita), bound for north Yorkshire to witness the first total eclipse of the sun for 200 years. The last leg of the journey was accomplished by coach to the top of Barden Fell above Richmond: 'Vales & moors stretched, slope after slope, round us. It was like the Haworth country.'[34] Here they joined a large crowd and awaited the event as the dawn broke. When the time came the early morning cloud dispersed as though by arrangement with some divine force, the air grew cold and the colours faded: 'I thought how we were like very old people, in the birth of the world – druids on Stonehenge.'[35] Then the colours returned to the land:

> – at first with a miraculous glittering and aetheriality, later normally almost, but with a great sense of relief. It was like recovery. We had been much worse than we had expected. We had seen the world dead.[36]

The nearest she had come previously to this strange country was in March 1921 on a train journey to Manchester through 'the great rocky moors'[37] of Derbyshire, another limestone landscape of bare craggy outcrops. On this occasion she was accompanying Leonard who had agreed to offer himself as Labour candidate for the Combined Universities. Memories of the soot-stained industrial city and its dreary academic life were soon dispelled by the 'bald moors'[38] of the Peak District:

> So solitary they might be 18th Century England, the valleys cut by a thread of water falling roughly from heights; great sweeps of country all sunny & gloomy with bare rocks against the sky, & then behold a row of east end slum houses, with a strip of pavement & two factory chimneys set down in the midst. ... Suddenly, in the palm of a wide valley you come on a complete town – gasworks, factories, and little streams made to run over stone steps & turn engines I suppose. Now & again no houses but wild moors, a thread of road, & farms set into the earth, uncompromising ...[39]

VII

EAST ANGLIA

A strange, lonely kind of country

Heraldic glass,
Blo' Norton Hall

In the summer of 1906 Virginia and Vanessa left London for a month in the country, staying on this occasion in a remote Elizabethan manor house on the Norfolk-Suffolk border. An American lady had taken a long lease on Blo' Norton Hall because, as Virginia wrote in her journal, 'it is too remote & solitary & ancestral for anyone to wish to live here, except Americans who find all these qualities, I suppose, medicinal.'[1] Miss Bancroft, a distant cousin of Henry James, was, however, happy to sub-let the hall for the whole of August and there, tucked away in the upper reaches of the Little Ouse valley and approached down a long avenue of lime trees, the Stephen sisters enjoyed 'a kind of honeymoon, interrupted it is true with horrible guests.'[2] On arrival along dusty lanes from Diss station, Virginia immediately felt herself soothed by a wonderful tranquillity:

Blo' Norton Hall
South front

79

... every mile seems to draw a thicker curtain than the last between you & the world. So that finally, when you are set down at the Hall, no sound what ever reaches your ear; the very light seems to filter through deep layers; & the air circulates slowly, as though it had but to make the circuit of the Hall, & its duties were complete.[3]

Chimney stack with Brampton datestone,

The hall with its wooded grounds and its moat was clearly to Virginia's liking. A terracotta panel set into one of the massive chimney stacks bears the date 1586 and the initials EHB, a reference to Elizabeth and Henry Brampton who enlarged the original timber frame building and added the pair of brick gables that were 'coloured like an apricot in the sun.'[4] The following day the two sisters set out to explore 'a strange, lonely kind of country'[5], an enchanted land that at first seemed both soporific and deserted:

The corn brims the fields, but no one is there to cut it; the churches hold up broad gray fingers all over the landscape, but no one, save perhaps the dead at their feet, attend to their commands; the windmills sail round & round, but no one trims their sails; it is very characteristic that the only sign of life in the land should be that produced by the wind of Heaven.[6]

Betty's Fen, Blo' Norton

Heraldic beast, Blo' Norton Hall staircase

Each day brought fresh discoveries. Blo' Norton is on the eastern edge of Breckland and there, just a mile from the hall, Virginia cultivated a preference for the great sweep of wild, melancholy heath that stretched westwards for miles without interruption. As she was soon to find out, once down in the valley the 'fen plays you false at every step'[7]. At the end of their second full day, a day spent stumbling through reeds, wading across ditches – 'the Little Ouse deserves its diminutive'[8] – and negotiating barbed wire fences, she decided the countryside did have possibilities but that although 'a walk in the fen has a singular charm, it is not to be undertaken as a way of getting to places.'[9] Later, in a letter to Violet Dickinson, she expressed her delight in both the hall and the surrounding countryside.

If only I had chosen a better time to write to you, I would describe this place. Which now I shant do. It is 300 years old, striped with oak bars inside, old staircases, ancestral vats and portraits; there is a garden; and a moat. You see people of taste can get houses cheap: the station is 6 miles off, & there is nothing to do. Nessa paints windmills in the afternoon, and I tramp the country for miles with a map, leap ditches, scale walls and desecrate churches, making out beautiful brilliant stories every step of the way. ...

Nessa and I have to go now and call on the Parson and we haven't been inside the church, even to sight see. Really this is a charming country, and even beautiful, or rather quaint as we say of things that are long and attenuated and more grotesque than shapely – because their hearts are so good.[10]

Not wishing to repeat their walk-in-the-fen experience quite so soon they decided on Hopton as their afternoon destination, a village on the Suffolk side of the valley approached more purposefully via a network of country lanes. '[T]hinking, arguing, & expounding'[11] all the way in the company of Thoby who, with brother Adrian was on a brief visit, Virginia still found time to pronounce upon the denominational allegiances of the local population:

... We passed the temples of three different sects, so that, reckoning by the number we met on the road there must be 10 orthodox Christians, 6 Methodists & $2^1/_2$ Anabaptists in Hopton. Children count only as halves, because when they grow up they may think for themselves, & swell the number of the hostile sect, or, presumably build a fresh chapel for themselves.[12]

The hall with screens passage and Gawdy Brampton portraits

On the return journey they paused at a crossroads and, mindful of her brother's imminent departure for Trieste, Virginia decided this was an appropriate parting of the ways: '... one road led straight to Dalmatia & the wilds of Thessaly; the other back here to this profound seat of solitude, dug, I think, somewhere very near the heart of England.'[13]

Dorothy Briscoe, second wife of Gawdy Brampton, d.1703

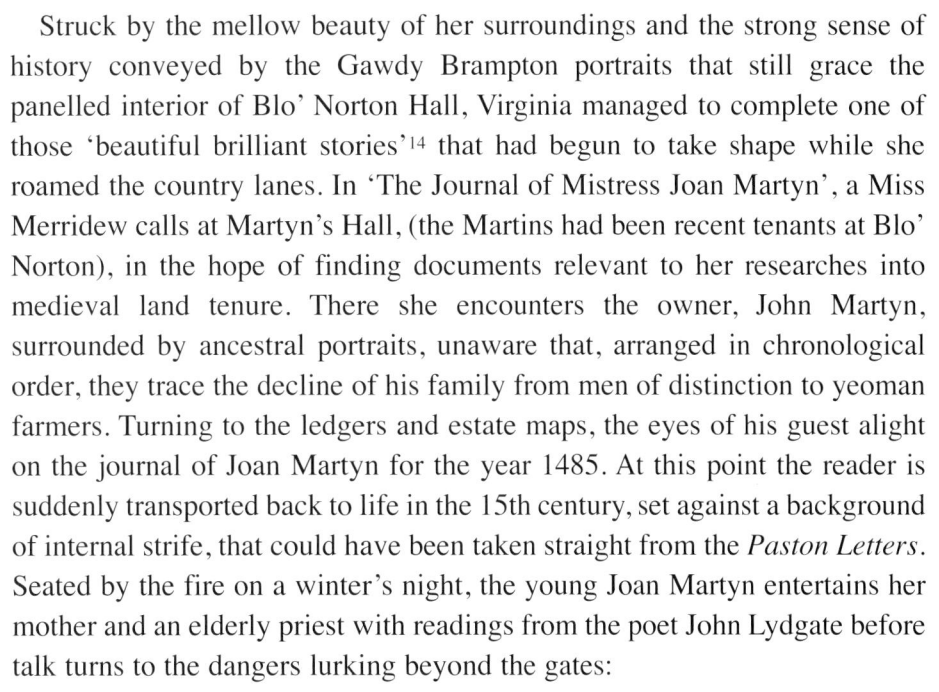

Struck by the mellow beauty of her surroundings and the strong sense of history conveyed by the Gawdy Brampton portraits that still grace the panelled interior of Blo' Norton Hall, Virginia managed to complete one of those 'beautiful brilliant stories'[14] that had begun to take shape while she roamed the country lanes. In 'The Journal of Mistress Joan Martyn', a Miss Merridew calls at Martyn's Hall, (the Martins had been recent tenants at Blo' Norton), in the hope of finding documents relevant to her researches into medieval land tenure. There she encounters the owner, John Martyn, surrounded by ancestral portraits, unaware that, arranged in chronological order, they trace the decline of his family from men of distinction to yeoman farmers. Turning to the ledgers and estate maps, the eyes of his guest alight on the journal of Joan Martyn for the year 1485. At this point the reader is suddenly transported back to life in the 15th century, set against a background of internal strife, that could have been taken straight from the *Paston Letters*. Seated by the fire on a winter's night, the young Joan Martyn entertains her mother and an elderly priest with readings from the poet John Lydgate before talk turns to the dangers lurking beyond the gates:

... when the time for bed comes, and the fire sinks, and we have to feel our way up the great stairs, and along the passages, where the windows shine grey, and so into our cold bed rooms. The window in my room is broken, and stuffed with straw, but gusts come in and lift the tapestry on the wall, till I think that horses and men in armour are charging down upon me. My prayer last night was, that the great gates might hold fast, and all robbers and murderers might pass us by.[15]

As a way of getting to places unscathed, Virginia took to the lanes on her bicycle and, intrigued by the site of a Saxon burial ground picked out in Gothick letters on her Ordnance Survey map, she set out for Kenninghall some five miles north of Blo' Norton. Her route took her through the village of Garboldisham and on past the gloomy Guiltcross workhouse 'for the care of the feeble minded', according to her map. Expecting earthworks as she approached Kenninghall, she began to enjoy the prospect of reclining 'upon such smooth turf'[16] in the manner of one familiar with the work of Richard Jefferies, the Wiltshire nature mystic. On arrival she soon discovered 'to the shame of Kenninghall'[17] that no one knew of its existence. Instead she found herself directed to the Christian burial ground skirting its medieval church beyond the market place where 'the curiously moulded tower, with its gilt clock, showed itself most decorously gray against the soft plumage of the trees.'[18]

Screens passage detail

Here she fell to musing on the literary possibilities of epitaphs because '... when you have exhausted the surface oddity, there is really a solid lump of truth to be dug out beneath.'[19] By way of illustration she jotted down this picture of a 'righteous old lady'[20] in St Mary's churchyard: 'She nothing took that plainness could not get/ and most abhorred [sic] the running into debt.'[21] Although the rows

c18 headstones, Kenninghall

of headstones have so far escaped the improving hand of churchyard maintenance the visitor in search of the inscription will look in vain, much as Virginia's search for interred Saxons ended in disappointment. The virtuous woman in question, one 'Mrs Susan Batt (shall we say)'[22] is perhaps so elusive because Virginia was less concerned for the precise details of local history than for the possibilities of a good story.

The pagan cemetery she sought had been excavated in 1869, well within living memory, and had yielded up a quantity of grave goods; weapons, beads and several cruciform brooches that suggest early Christian influence here. Rather than admit defeat, Virginia decided to 'consecrate a mound in some gentleman's Park'[23], unaware that the burial ground she sought lay unannounced beneath a ploughed field just yards from where she stood at the entrance to the Quidenham estate. Contemplating the mound from the park gate she 'could see no reason why Saxons should not have been buried there.'[24] Closer inspection would have revealed nothing earlier than an eighteenth century ice-house, but, late in the day, it satisfied Virginia's flagging curiosity.

Icehouse, Quidenham Park

Had she cycled a little further along the Quidenham road she might have discovered a more celebrated earthwork. Identified on her map as 'Vikings' Mound', it is almost certainly a Norman castle motte but the people of Quidenham too have refused to allow history to stand in the way of a good story. The discovery of a large quantity of bones in the churchyard opposite soon gave rise to the tradition of a battle fought nearby in the reign of Queen Boudica and since then 'Vikings' Mound' has always been known locally as the grave of England's most famous revolutionary heroine. Unlike their Kenninghall neighbours, left to ponder a few self-righteous epitaphs, Quidenham knew how to honour its dead. Virginia, whose idea for an article on gravestone verse never got beyond the pages of her journal might well have applauded Quidenham's more imaginative endeavours.

Undeterred by her trip to Kenninghall she consulted the guidebook once more and decided that Thetford, with its legacy of monastic ruins, offered a more rewarding prospect to the discerning traveller in search of the picturesque. Since her arrival in Norfolk nearly a month before, the countryside had been transformed. As she set out on a scorching hot day through a landscape with harvest in full swing and the air 'rich with energy and brilliant with colour,'[25] she offers her imaginary readers a series of images which, by her own admission, she is too lazy to compose into a picture:

> ... a bare road across a moor, fields of corn & stubble – a haze as of wood fire smoke – innumerable pheasants & partridges – white stones – thatched cottages – sign posts – tiny villages – great waggons heaped with corn – sagacious dogs, farmers carts.[26]

'The smooth turf slope' of Castle Hill, Thetford

Situated at the confluence of the Thet and Little Ouse rivers Thetford has a long and noble history for what, in 1906, was a small, rather sleepy market town. It was once a thriving Saxon burgh; centre of the East Anglian bishopric in the 11th century and a major religious centre following the foundation of a Cluniac priory, with several monastic houses and no less than 22 medieval churches. When, after an hour's ride across open heathland,

Virginia dropped down into the welcome shade of the river valley she was at once greeted by earthworks that more than made up for the disappointment of Kenninghall. Only Silbury Hill in Wiltshire rises to a greater height than the conical mound known as Castle Hill. Its origins have been variously assigned to every successive invasion since the Celts but it is now clear that the Normans raised a defensive motte from within the ramparts of an Iron Age fort at a point where the old Icknield Way crossed the Little Ouse. It may well have been the military centre from which Boudica launched her rebellion against the Romans.

Thetford with its 'girdle of wall & river, & the smooth turf slope outside'[27] seemed to Virginia rather like an Italian town, a comparison prompted in part by the ruins of a nunnery mentioned in her guide book and by the sight of a Roman Catholic priest, complete with biretta, emerging from his door. The remains of St George's nunnery, founded by monks from Bury St Edmunds, lie a short distance south of Castle Hill over one of the stone bridges 'where anglers lounged'.[28] Exhausted by the ride and mesmerised by the river, she found herself questioning the reality of the scene that drifted before her eyes:

> No one was ever able to say exactly what does go on in these medieval towns set in the heart of England at about this hour on a Summers afternoon. ... For when you come upon stalwart men leaning their elbows on a parapet & dreaming of the stream beneath ... you reconsider what you mean by life. Often in London shall I think of Thetford, & wonder if it is still alive; or whether it has really ceased, peaceably, to exist any longer. No one would notice if the whole town forgot to wake up one morning.[29]

Melford Bridge, 1697, on the outskirts of Thetford

There was no immediate cause for concern. Thetford slumbered on until, in the 1960s, it was rudely awakened by the sound of London overspill. Brash new shopping streets ripped the heart out of its historic centre but along the river bank visitors may still enjoy the tree-lined path known as Spring Walk laid out as part of an attempt to promote Thetford as a spa town in the early 19th century. The Nunnery is today safe in the hands of the British Trust for Ornithology and Castle Hill, no longer grazed by sheep, remains a dramatic reminder of the town's more turbulent past.

Four miles south west of Thetford on the main London road lies the village of Elveden, centre of Lord Iveagh's huge Breckland estate, acquired by the head of the Guinness dynasty just a few years before Virginia's holiday in the Little Ouse valley. The name Elvedon Hall which she used in *The Waves* (1925) for the secret world of privilege glimpsed by Bernard and Susan over its park wall, has led to speculation that she was familiar with the Suffolk mansion from her time at Blo'Norton. But Lord Iveagh's palatial residence, in almost flat parkland and invisible from the road, bears no relation to the author's invention, a white house set in a deep hollow among trees. Although her diary for the summer of 1906 is incomplete she is unlikely to have visited

Elveden Hall

such an extraordinary building without mention. As Bernard explains – 'I have seen signposts at the cross-roads with one arm pointing "To Elvedon"'[30] – and the author too is more likely either to have seen directions while cycling to Thetford or the name on her OS map confirming the existence of a hall set in parkland and a name with imaginative possibilities. The derivation of Elveden from the Old English 'elfel-denu' or 'swan valley' is less prosaic than might be expected, but in *The Waves* its suggestion of elves and eden would enhance the hall's ambiguous status as a place both real and imagined.

The historical investigations undertaken by the narrator in 'The Journal of Mistress Joan Martyn' anticipate with remarkable accuracy both the imminent arrival and the antiquarian interests of Blo' Norton's most celebrated resident, an Indian prince with strong family links to Elveden. The Maharajah Duleep Singh had purchased the Elveden estate in 1863 with money from the British government and the 'Black Prince', as he became known in the area, enlarged the modest Georgian hall into an Oriental extravaganza covered in Carrara marble. His son, Prince Frederick, a Cambridge-educated historian fascinated by all aspects of Norfolk's past, lived locally at Old Buckenham Hall before achieving his ambition to secure a long lease on Blo' Norton Hall. Virginia would not have been aware of the new tenant – he did not arrive until 1909, but in *The Waves* (1931) 'The gardener with the black beard'[31] who catches sight of the children leaning over the wall at Elvedon may have been a sly reference to his association with Blo' Norton.

Ancient House Museum, given to Thetford by Prince Frederick

Prince Frederick was conservative by nature, declining to install electricity or telephone, and sympathetic to the Jacobite cause. Blo' Norton Hall was adorned with portraits of Bonnie Prince Charlie while a painting of Cromwell hung upside down. His collection of Stuart relics included a pendant containing a piece of the block on which Charles I was executed and a locket with a ringlet of the monarch's hair. His layout of the grounds incorporated a pillared temple in a wood dedicated to 'The Divine Winds of Heaven', those same 'wind[s] of Heaven'[32] powering unattended windmills that Virginia found so engaging on her arrival. Among his acts of generosity the Prince purchased a richly carved medieval merchant's house in Thetford, one of those 'curious old houses'[33] noted by Virginia on her visit, and gave it to the town as a museum. He remained at Blo' Norton until his death in 1926 and is buried in the churchyard.

Thelnetham windmill opposite Blo' Norton Hall

Although much has changed since Virginia's stay over a century ago, the hall, with its screens passage, Jacobean staircase and family portraits, still manages to convey an atmosphere of ancestral well-being. Rooted deep in the East Anglian countryside and weighed down by the past the house peers out across open fields where 'landmarks resolve themselves into churches

& windmills'.[34] Restored to working order and clearly visible through the trees stands Thelnetham corn mill, an early 19th century brick tower mill and one of the features by which Virginia attempted to navigate her way through the intervening fen, but today there is far less chance of getting lost in the reed beds. Much of this marshy terrain, once a common feature of the Little Ouse valley, has disappeared beneath the plough leaving a few isolated remnants where it is still possible to wander 'into a lush fen, humming with dragonflies & scented with meadow sweet.'[35] At Market Weston Fen, managed by the Suffolk Wildlife Trust, fragrant orchid and round leaved sundew thrive in the boggy conditions and a little further east Redgrave and Lopham Fen is home to the rare great raft spider. Here or on the heath at Knettishall or cycling past the ruined church at Gasthorpe on a hot summer day it is possible to revisit that same 'strange, grey green, undulating, dreaming, philosophising & remembering land'[36] that Virginia found so enchanting.

Gasthorpe ruined church near Blo' Norton

As Mrs Woolf, Virginia returned briefly to East Anglia on several occasions, but Blo' Norton was to provide her most cherished memories of the region. No stretch of coastline could rival her beloved Cornwall and during the Woolfs' short stay on the Suffolk coast in June 1912 just before their marriage, the dreary expanse of shingle and low, crumbling cliffs failed to win her lasting affection. Recalling the visit years later in a letter to Violet Dickinson she wrote with obvious displeasure: 'Why do you stay at Aldeburgh, there are east winds there, both of God and man'[37] and later referred to it as 'that miserable, dull, sea village' very much in the style of its most famous son, the poet George Crabbe.

Aldeburgh

Walberswick, where the Woolfs had stayed at the Bell Inn, was already something of an artists' colony following the success of Wilson Steer's dazzling series of Impressionist beach scenes completed in the 1880s. The transformation from fishing village to holiday retreat for the middle classes was ironically already reshaping the St Ives of Virginia's childhood, but here in Suffolk her irritation with this self-consciously picturesque place and the amateur attempts to commit it to canvas persisted. Years later writing to thank her friend Margaret Llewelyn Davies for some gift of embroidery she enquired:

> How did it come to Walberswick? Don't tell me that its the product of one of those little artistic cottages which used to annoy us so – I dont want to credit the artists of Walberswick with any decent feelings.[38]

The nearest Virginia came to establishing a more lasting association with the region was in 1916 when Vanessa, along with Duncan Grant and David ('Bunny') Garnett, went to stay at Wissett Lodge near Halesworth, made vacant by the death of Grant's aunt. Here the young men hoped to gain exemption from military service on the strength of re-establishing the fruit garden and the orchard. Virginia relayed the news to Ka Cox:

You have heard how Duncan has become a fruit farmer in Suffolk with Bunny Garnett? He came up after a week of it and says he finds it very soothing, and all his faculties sink to sleep. He is out picking Big Bug off the currant bushes for 8 hours a day: sleeps all night, paints on Sundays. ... Nessa is going to keep house for him perhaps all summer. So you see, Bloomsbury is vanished like the morning mist.[39]

Wissett Lodge

In July the Woolfs went to stay at Wissett. Writing at the end of the month to Lytton Strachey who had returned from his own visit several weeks earlier, Virginia declared: 'Wissett seems to lull asleep all ambition – Don't you think they have discovered the secret of life? I thought it wonderfully harmonious.'[40] And to Vanessa: 'I've seldom enjoyed myself more than I did with you, and I can't make out exactly how you manage. One seems to get into such a contented state of mind.'[41] She then confided: 'I am very much interested in your life, which I think of writing another novel about. Its fatal staying with you – you start so many new ideas.'[42] This was Virginia's first reference to her idea for *Night and Day* in which Katherine Hilbery, daughter of a famous literary family, is modelled on Vanessa. The soporific atmosphere induced by the Suffolk countryside in high summer was soon dispelled by an unsympathetic tribunal hearing in Halesworth that persuaded Grant and Garnett to leave for Sussex and Charleston. Here, by finding more gainful employment on a local farm, they deprived Wissett of a more permanent place in the history of Bloomsbury.

The 'mediaeval picture' of Stiffkey Old Hall and church

The salt marshes and great estates of north Norfolk presented Virginia with a remote, ancestral landscape more to her liking when in March 1932, following a trip to Cambridge, the Woolfs decided to explore the 'lovely, lonely coast'[43] between King's Lynn and Cromer. Stiffkey Hall with its gatehouse and cluster of circular flint towers beside the church appeared 'as in a mediaeval picture'[44] on rising ground above the chalk stream from which the village takes its name and the whole scene put her in mind of the Pastons. Throughout their stay this empty landscape with its 'lovely stubborn unknown place names; & wild roads'[45] was haunted by Dora Carrington's recent suicide and Virginia's attempts to make sense of it. The end of her diary entry for March 17th is all the more poignant for its brevity: '... the name Partridge of course appearing on tombs & grocers' shops'[46] everywhere they went.

It seems clear from her essay 'The Pastons and Chaucer' (1925) that Virginia was not only familiar with the letters, assembled by James Gairdner and first published in 1904, but with the landscape of north east Norfolk –

'the most desolate part of England known to us at the present moment.'[47] Although there is no reference to a visit here she brings both the time and the place so alive that a fleeting visit for research purposes may have gone unrecorded. In September 1905 she was urging Emma Vaughan to make her own pilgrimage to Paston.

Caister Castle,
Early c19 engraving,

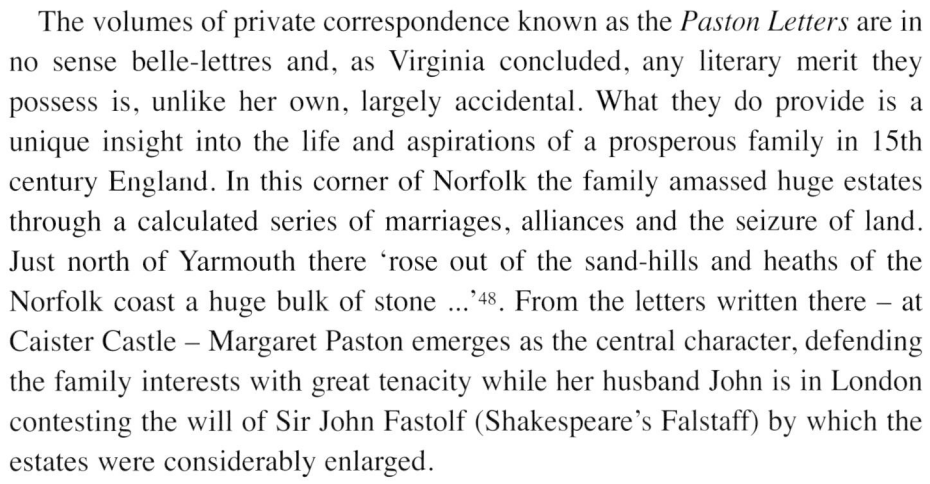

The volumes of private correspondence known as the *Paston Letters* are in no sense belle-lettres and, as Virginia concluded, any literary merit they possess is, unlike her own, largely accidental. What they do provide is a unique insight into the life and aspirations of a prosperous family in 15th century England. In this corner of Norfolk the family amassed huge estates through a calculated series of marriages, alliances and the seizure of land. Just north of Yarmouth there 'rose out of the sand-hills and heaths of the Norfolk coast a huge bulk of stone ...'[48]. From the letters written there – at Caister Castle – Margaret Paston emerges as the central character, defending the family interests with great tenacity while her husband John is in London contesting the will of Sir John Fastolf (Shakespeare's Falstaff) by which the estates were considerably enlarged.

A few miles up the coast, approached through the ruins of its medieval gatehouse, the remains of Bromholm Priory lie scattered in a farmyard. With a piece of the true Cross in its possession the priory had been one of the great centres of monastic life. Chaucer's reeve swore 'by the Holy Cross of Bromholm' and the precious relic attracted pilgrims to this remote outpost of

Remains of south transept,
Broomholm Priory

Christianity 'and sent them away with eyes opened and limbs straightened.'[49] The body of John Paston was brought here for burial and '[t]wo panes were taken from the church windows to let out the reek of the torches'[50] but his grave lay unmarked for several years. A mile or so distant, huddled together against the bitter onshore winds, stand the church, the tithe barn and the hall in the village from which the Pastons took their name. It was here in 1466 that John Paston's body was finally laid to rest beneath a table tomb in the chancel of St Margaret's church.

Sir William Paston's tithe barn, 1581

Today little survives of the dynasty which flourished for 300 years. Caister Castle, presently a museum celebrating the achievements of the motor car, is just a fragment of the moated and fortified house that once extended over six acres: 'now jackdaws nest on the tower ... Antiquaries speculate and differ'[51] and over this corner of Norfolk where the Pastons once ruled:

... broods a sense of discomfort and nakedness; of unwashed limbs thrust into splendid clothing; of tapestry blowing on the draughty walls; of the bedroom with its privy; of winds sweeping straight over land unmitigated by hedge or town; ... and of the plain-faced Pastons indefatigably accumulating wealth, treading out the roads of Norfolk, and persisting with an obstinate courage which does them infinite credit in furnishing the bareness of England.[52]

VIII

RYE and ROMNEY MARSH

*All the land around was
black and turbulent as the sea*

In the months following Virginia's 'kind of honeymoon'[1] with Vanessa on the Norfolk/Suffolk border two events occurred that were to redefine their relationship. A year later, in 1907, when Virginia decided to take a house near Rye for the summer, she was still recovering from the loss of their brother Thoby who had died suddenly of typhoid fever in November of the previous year. Two days after the tragedy Vanessa had agreed to marry Clive Bell. Although the sisters continued to take holidays together they never again recaptured the magic of Blo' Norton Hall or the shared intimacy of that summer. Virginia and her younger brother Adrian had been offered a house in

Curfew Cottage

Playden by a Mrs Dew-Smith through Virginia's friendship with Gwen Raverat. They arrived at The Steps in early August. Two weeks later the Bells, who had been visiting Clive's family in Wiltshire, took up residence in the centre of Rye at Curfew Cottage in Watchbell Street, but as Virginia confided to Violet Dickinson '... of sister there is less than there used to be.'[2]

Adrian and Virginia on the lawn of The Steps, c.1908, Vanessa Bell

The Steps, now but a ghostly reminder of the house in which Virginia stayed, was much newer than the tall Regency-style villa suggested by Vanessa's painting and seemed to satisfy Virginia's simple requirements; 'we have a real country cottage – white walls, and bright pictures, and cheerful manly books, Stevenson and Thoreau, and a garden and an orchard'.[3] The house had, however, been taken primarily for its position rather than any claim to antiquity, perched on the side of a hill above Rye with the expanse of Romney Marsh stretching away to the sea. Once installed Virginia was soon writing enthusiastically to Lady Cecil:

This comes of sitting all day, before a tremendous view, flat as sand; the sea once came right up to the foot of the Cliff on which this house is built; now it has withdrawn, and instead of bleached bones, and the ribs of ships hung with weed, there are sheep, and cottages and cornfields.[4]

Crowned for some distance by the squat weather-vaned tower of St Mary's church, the little hill town of Rye, 'bristling with red roofs & chimneys,'[5] rises from the marsh as though transposed from a medieval painting perhaps or stranded like some enormous sea urchin by the outgoing tide. The great storm of 1287 that drowned Old Winchelsea had diverted the course of the Rother so that it flowed out to sea at Rye, gradually destroying the lower parts of the town. On Speede's 1616 map of Sussex, Rye is still virtually an island surrounded on three sides by the estuarine waters of the Rother and its tributary the Brede, but by then the waters had already begun to recede choking the harbour with silt.

Dutch School view of Rye from the north, c.1730

On closer inspection the steep slopes of the town appear, covered by a breathtaking sequence of old buildings. Solid brick houses slotted in between weatherboarded and heavily beamed cottages are crammed together around a web of narrow cobble streets that converge on Church Square. Arranged at intervals around the edge the remains of the town's fortifications – the Ypres Tower, Landgate and sections of its curtain wall – are reminders of a more turbulent past. Throughout the Middle Ages this stretch of the south coast remained vulnerable to attack not just from the sea but from the French. Despite its membership of the Cinque Ports, a defensive confederation of towns along the Kent and Sussex coastline, Rye was sacked on several occasions culminating in the conflagration of 1377 that destroyed most of the town.

Mermaid Street

Confronted by a past so reverently preserved, Virginia refused to be intimidated by the Antient Town but did confess to 'a little weariness of all brick & mortar, that is steeped in history.'[6] Her reaction to the place was shaped in part by the considerable presence of Henry James and the prospect of taking tea with the distinguished author. James had moved here from London in 1898 on the strength of a watercolour in a friend's house depicting the garden room annexed to Lamb House, and set about acquiring the most imposing residence in Rye 'on terms quite deliciously moderate.' Situated on a corner of West Street with a view to the church and a flourishing walled garden, this handsome Georgian town house appealed to the American's taste and sense of tradition. James had been a good friend of Leslie Stephen and continued to take a paternal interest in his children, an interest that seldom

Henry James,
John Singer Sargent, 1913

extended beyond disapproval of Virginia's bohemian ways or the appearance of friends like Lytton Strachey and Saxon Sydney-Turner who were staying close by with Vanessa and 'that little image' Clive Bell.

Having reviewed *The Golden Bowl* for the *Guardian* in February 1905 Virginia was already familiar with the writer's work and clearly had the measure of his style. In her letter to Lady Cecil she complained: 'I am embalmed in a book of Henry James: The American Scene: like a fly in amber. I dont expect to get out; but it is very quiet and luminous.'[7] She did not however consider it 'the stuff of genius: no it should be a swift stream'[8] rather than the sluggish meanderings of the Rother. In a letter to Violet Dickinson she recalls the obligatory visit to the great writer who regaled his company with 'all the scandal of Rye'[9]. This was followed by an amusing verbatim account of his discourse, delivered in the High Street, on discovering that Virginia too was a writer, while his guests shuffled nervously on the pavement.

The Garden Room
Lamb House, Edward Warren

Rye, antiquated and exhausting, became forever associated with Henry James and although Virginia continued to review his work their paths seldom crossed again. James remained in the town, a large shadowy figure, until his death in 1916 and his unfinished work *The Sense of the Past* was, indirectly,

ENGLISH HOURS

a measure of the affection in which he held the place. In the same year Bloomsbury, for whom the gentility of Rye held no such appeal, took up residence in a large, draughty farmhouse at the foot of the South Downs. Lamb House was subsequently leased to the author EF Benson until in August 1940 a bomb destroyed the garden room where James had written many of his novels. Ten years later the property was acquired by the National Trust and, like the rest of the town, it too has become embalmed.

At Blo' Norton Virginia and Vanessa had spent much of their time leaping ditches and tramping the heath but now with her sister several months pregnant, Virginia had come to Sussex intent on the serious business of reviewing for the national press. Here her customary enthusiasm for the countryside was less evident and, as this first entry in her journal (Aug. 1907) makes clear, she came determined to see it in a different light:

Plaque on the garden wall, Lamb House

> It requires more imagination though, not to read history into the land than to see a blank sheet of hill & valley. For Sussex soil has been turned infinitely often, has been smoothed like a coverlet, over graves, over seeds, has been rolled & raked & baked finally into those ripe old houses which are so lavish of their information. And yet we did not come to the country to listen to venerable gossip over tea cups; no; we came to hear certain melancholy birds who have learnt only the one cry ... We came to see the land that has kept its own counsel, obeyed its own will, since the day it carved itself thus, before any gave it name or likeness.[10]

The Dyke by the Road, 1922, woodcut, Paul Nash

Rye Harbour, watercolour, c.1938, Eric Ravilious

With a growing confidence in her ability to write and with excursions restricted to a gentle evening stroll, Virginia became more pre-occupied with the atmospheric effects of light and the dissolution of form. On one evening Virginia and Adrian were out on the terrace at Playden under the stars. Great hawk-moths hovered over the tobacco plants that gleamed in the moonlight, 'their fine perfume powdered the air with sweetness'.[11] As they sat marvelling at the immensity of the universe the distant sound of drums and a trumpet, suggesting a fair, drifted up from Rye and the two decided to set off downhill to investigate. Having failed to locate the source of the music they took the road home that skirted the marsh. 'The flats glistened beneath the moon, & there were odd smooth barns by the wayside, all dark, like colour shapes in some 18th century watercolour.'[12] The silence, broken only by the eerie cry of a marsh bird or the cough of a sheep, was soon shattered by 'a great luminous train, semi transparent, [that] came rattling before us; with a body like some phosphorescent caterpillar, & a curled plume of smoke, all opal & white ...'[13]

Virginia's journal entry for September 3rd is a summation of several walks in the half light and is presented as a series of landscape meditations. From a raised platform on Rye's town wall beside the Ypres Tower she stood and observed the effect of the sun setting behind Winchelsea:

... staining all that steep space of air & chequering the marsh land with liquid yellows, & mellow shadows ... The mounds, or cliffs, – you cant call them hills, so sudden & unexpected are they, solidify as evening draws on, & make great soft blots on the landscape, otherwise so wide & simple. And then the sea is still there to the South, hoarding the last blue, & still going about its business, carrying ruddy fishing boats, & all the busy craft of steamers.[14]

During the reign of Henry VIII the French still posed a considerable threat along the south coast and Camber Castle, on the levels between Rye and Winchelsea, is one of five polygonal block houses built around 1540 to guard against invasion. Abandoned by the sea and approached along a farm track this massive bastion has spread itself over the turf like some monumental folly, its rounded ashlar face scarred not by enemy fire – it was never used in anger – but by the corrosive action of the salt-laden air. Virginia walked here in the fading light through fields of 'pearl white sheep,'[15] the land around bathed in 'a certain transparent lucidity.'[16] She noted the effect of the castle's grey stone walls 'against a sky of scarlet plumes,'[17] how the peculiar light blurred the rough surface and how, in the rising mist, '[t]he ring of castle wall holds in the heat, like a cup brimming with soft vapours.'[18]

Camber Castle

Rising above the intervening meadows Winchelsea's 'sombre mound'[19], crowned by the barrel of its weatherboarded mill 'grew almost ink black, with those deep liquid shadows'[20] and was already 'sunk into the dark layers of its foliage.'[21] The day had been wild and now the 'clouds shift, drag apart, & go in tattered sheets hanging down with frayed edges right across the landscape.'[22] From this low point of reference on the marsh the perspective shifts and the mood changes. The waters appear to rise under cover of darkness and reclaim the land. Rye's diminutive hill has become a funereal mound while:

> All the land all round was black & turbulent as the sea; ... it seemed as though the air itself was all broken & confused, a shattered medium, no longer a tranquil void for clouds to sail in. The river lay quite pale at the base of the hill; the clearest & most peaceful thing in the landscape.[23]

Brangwyn's post mill,
Winchelsea,
Adrian Hill, c.1940

Each year towards the end of September Virginia detected a subtle change in atmosphere that signalled the end of summer and a return to London. The land became drained of colour and the wind blew more purposefully but, as she observed; '... on a generous day, no light is lovelier, warmer, more melancholy; as of some perpetual afternoon.'[24] In the Fens this change, recorded in her Warboys Journal, was marked by the lighting of bonfires and a new sharpness in the air while here, in this chequerboard of orchards and hop fields, the onset of autumn was determined more precisely:

> September here means that the poles are stripped naked of the garlands of hops. Indeed a hop field is a graceful place, sweetly planted with alleys, & laced across with

105

tender green ribbons; the earth is all flecked yellow & green & you walk beneath shade. Now I say, this has gone, as though beneath the blast of a storm ...[25]

Despite her irritation with the picturesque excesses of a landscape dotted with tile-hung farmhouses, she first considered the idea of a writer's retreat in Sussex while here on a visit to Peasmarsh, a village submerged in apple orchards three miles west of Playden. Seduced by 'all the vague scents & coolnesses of a country evening washing over one's body'[26] she found the smallest of cottages with 'thick walls, & robust floors'[27] just off the road. To own such a place would, she thought, give her great pleasure back in Fitzroy Square knowing that 'it lies moored there, ready for us to embark upon.'[28] She could imagine the lamp in the window and how 'I shall tramp up the flagged path; and see my chair ready, the table spread ... '[29]. Over the next few years this fanciful notion took shape until Virginia decided to lease a cottage in Firle (see Chapt. XI), the first of several properties in Sussex that began her long, romantic attachment to the county.

The Landgate, Rye

IX
SOMERSET

Wave like hills ... episcopal swans ... middle class bicyclists

When, in August 1908, Vanessa and Clive Bell went to stay with his family at Cleeve House near the Wiltshire town of Devizes, Virginia decided to travel down to the West Country in order to be near her sister. Marlborough, just 10 miles south of Devizes, would have been ideal but, fearing a proposal of marriage from Hilton Young, a contemporary of Thoby's at Cambridge, she declined his invitation to stay, preferring the cloistered seclusion of Wells in Somerset. Here she hoped to make progress on 'Melymbrosia', her first novel eventually published as *The Voyage Out* in 1915.

As the novelist Sylvia Townsend Warner found when writing her county guide forty years later, it is often difficult to decide whether Somerset is 'a flat county with a quantity of hills in it or a hilly county of which a great deal is as level as a pavement. Like a shot silk, it depends which way you look at it.'[1]

Wells Cathedral below the Mendips

ENGLISH HOURS

Wells, the epitome of the small cathedral city, had spread itself comfortably below the Mendips where several wooded coombs converge. Arriving by train from London on a warm summer evening in 1908, Virginia expressed her pleasure in the surrounding countryside: 'I was delighted by the little wave like hills which seemed to form all round me; to culminate in one high mound, upon which stood the oblong of Glastonbury Tor.'[2] Rather like Wells itself 'Somerset farm houses are built of grey stone, are of great age, have a way of backing into some recess at the base of a down, as though to make room for the flat lawn, protected by a wall, which generally lies before them. They are sheltered places.'[3]

West front, Wells Cathedral

Violet Dickinson, whose grandfather had been bishop of Bath and Wells, had found lodgings for Virginia in the Close but her choice of cathedral city may also have been influenced by her reading of Henry James. His travel essays, written while touring through some of this country's beauty spots in the late 19th century, had first appeared in a number of East Coast literary journals and a selection had recently been published in Britain under the title *English Hours* (1905). Although she does not refer to the collection directly, James was a family friend and she was already well acquainted with his work.

Vicars' Close

In 1872 James, like Virginia, still in his twenties, had stopped off in Wells on his way back from a trip to north Devon. Arriving late in the day he quickly set out to explore the town: 'it is a cathedral with a little city gathered at the base and forming hardly more than an extension of the spacious close. You feel everywhere the presence of the beautiful church; the place seems always to savour of a Sunday afternoon.'[4] Gazing up at the celebrated west front, its rows of bishops, saints and kings 'densely embroidered by the chisel,'[5] the cathedral seemed 'less a temple for man's needs than a monument of his pride.'[6] The theatrical possibilities of Vicars' Close, built in the mid-14th century to house a congregation of minor clergy, appealed more to his imagination:

The place is adorably of another world and time, and, approaching it as I did in the first dimness of twilight, it looked to me, in its exaggerated perspective, like one of those conventional streets represented on the stage, down whose impossible vista the heroes and confidants of romantic comedies come swaggering arm-in-arm and hold amorous converse with heroines perched at second-storey windows.[7]

As Virginia found, life in the Close was not so far removed from James' fanciful picture and could be distracting on a hot August day: 'old ladies chatter their gossip across the Close, and love making begins with the rise of the moon,'[8] but as she concluded, 'passion is proper to the season.'[9] At first she seemed well pleased with her lodgings in Vicars' Close announcing to Clive Bell 'I am in the midst of ecclesiasticism here.'[10] The owner and widow of a railway guard, Mrs Wall had lived in the Close for the last thirty years, had raised ten children and had been surrogate mother to countless young theological students she liked to refer to as her gentlemen. 'Never was there a more amiable, useful old creature.'[11]

Once installed Virginia set out to explore the place, discovering first the Bishop's Palace south of the cloisters – 'Certain night walks have shown me battlements & a moat; ...'[12]. Wandering through the medieval gateway known as Penniless Porch she came to the Market Place: 'there is a stately square, which, when I first saw it, was crowded with farmers, listening in a circle, to the vociferations of a little old man in a cap & gown'.[13] Apart from these brief observations, she had little to say about the architectural delights of Wells and appears not to have set foot inside the Cathedral during her two week stay. She had come to write but, despite the impression of peace and serenity that first strikes the visitor, daily life soon proved more noisy than the aspiring novelist had anticipated. Musical clerics, singing curates and tradesmen banging on the door were bad enough but the prospect of a return invitation from the shy theological student upstairs with whom she had already spent

Cathedral Green

one tedious evening, finally persuaded Virginia to move into rooms overlooking Cathedral Green.

The house, once prosperous but now 'rather shabby & threadbare'[14], was overshadowed by an enormous tree that obscured any view of the cathedral and contributed to an atmosphere of baronial gloom: 'A candle has to burn perpetually in a corner, to illumine the steep stairs; which have bannisters of carved oak & great oaken balls at the landing.'[15] Her new lodgings were no more conducive to writing and it was not long before she became exasperated by the noise of children outside her window:

> The Cathedral Green is rather spent by the time it reaches this far corner, & the grass, upon which you may not walk, elsewhere, seems here to lose its sacred character & to become a playground of the children of the neighbouring houses.[16]

Shrieks from the two resident children in the flat below exhausted her patience and attempts to remonstrate with the parents proved equally frustrating. 'The man has an impediment'[17] she complained to Clive Bell 'which makes him repeat all he says twice over, and the woman is deaf, so that I have to repeat all I say twice over.'[18] Despite fretting over names for several female characters and numerous distractions Virginia managed to make some headway with her novel and, returning from a tramp over the Mendips one Sunday in forgiving mood, she felt able to write: 'All the bells ringing, and the fashion of Wells parading before me. It is a lovely place, and the country round is as good as it can be.'[19]

As a respite from writing and the distractions of the Close, Virginia took to the hills each day with her dogs Hans and Gurth. On one occasion, exhilarated by the exercise, the changing prospect of the Somerset Levels spread out below her elicited an outburst which, for its patriotic fervour, echoed Stephen Womack's response to the Wiltshire downs in EM Forster's *The Longest Journey* published the previous year:

> ... all the air was hung with tattered clouds ... the most beautiful sky there is, perhaps; it is always moving, always letting through different lights & shades on to the land below. It is a wide land, uneasy, like the sea, full of mounds, & high lines into the horizon. When the sun gleamed, great bones of green & brown earth showed in the middle of this scene, which was coloured like some drawing in brown ink. The kingdoms of the world lay before me, a rich domain teeming in the folds with apples, & meadows, with gray villages snug in hollows, & little steeples. Far away the sea,

Cathedral west front (detail)

into which the land may spill its treasure. ... this view stands for many I suppose, as a symbol of their mother England ...[20]

On another day, returning wet and dishevelled to the genteel calm of the Close, Virginia seemed to revel in a certain notoriety: 'my appearance, when I have been on the downs in a shower, and jumped a ditch on the way home, delights the people of Wells – draws a smile even from their Bishop.'[21] This uneasy truce was shattered the following Sunday when her dogs leapt into the bishop's moat in pursuit of 'the episcopal swans and ducks, to the consternation of the inhabitants.'[22] Shortly after they escaped once more and ran wild in the town before being apprehended by a policeman.

Bishop's palace gatehouse

Seldom comfortable as a tourist in the conventional sense, Virginia soon regretted her brief excursions to two of Somerset's most popular attractions. 'I have been horribly disabused by visiting Glastonbury and Cheddar'[23] she complained to Saxon Sydney-Turner, 'the populace was disgusting as usual.'[24] Appalled by the cheap commercialism that even then had begun to blight its craggy face, she confided to Vanessa that Cheddar was 'a wretched place, like the scenery beside a switch back, crowded, and full of grottoes and caves, into which I could not bother to look.'[25] Her spirits, already brought low by the experience, might have revived on the journey back to Wells but for an unscheduled stop to enable a little girl, terrified by a drunk passenger, to be transferred to her compartment. Disturbed by the intrusion, Virginia appears to have made no attempt to console the child who '... was like a frightened rabbit, and crouched in her corner.'[26]

If Cheddar seemed cheap and vulgar the ruins of Glastonbury's great monastic shrine were in danger of being transformed into a municipal park. This, once the richest foundation in Britain outside Westminster Abbey, had been revered throughout the Christian world as the resting place of St Dunstan, several Saxon kings and a number of Celtic saints. When in 1190 monks claimed to have uncovered the graves of Arthur and Guinevere, the Abbey's reputation as a place of pilgrimage remained unrivalled until the Dissolution. By the time of Virginia's visit, despite the ravages of time, it was almost as though the great edifice had finally collapsed under the great weight of tradition heaped upon it. Today the romance of the past still sits uneasily with the commercial reality of the present. The place retains little of its magic and, as Virginia suggested, it is perhaps better to leave Glastonbury to the imagination and go no further:

> It was dark and windy; I missed the ruins, and found them, and thought them not half as good as the Glastonbury I have had in my head. They are too clean, and too dilapidated; besides new scaffolding is all over them, and there are benches at the proper views, notices about the sacred building; and middle class bicyclists resting their ugly bodies all over the place ... who wants to discover more stone pillars of mutilated Early English architecture![27]

Abbey ruins, Glastonbury

ENGLISH HOURS

The problem had begun two years earlier when the ruins were acquired by the Church of England and the inevitable process of preservation began. When Henry James had explored them twenty five years earlier they were still delightfully picturesque:

> ... the dainty weeds and wild flowers overlace the antique tracery with their bright arabesques and deepen the gray of the stone-work as it brightens their bloom. The thousand flowers which grow among English ruins deserve a chapter to themselves ... [28]

By the time Sylvia Townsend Warner wrote her *Somerset* in 1949 the ruins were, she conceded, still beautiful, adding slyly 'no grass could be greener or smoother'[29] but echoed the disappointment of many including Virginia. 'It is almost impossible to conjure up the vivacity and energy of a great medieval abbey in surroundings so respectfully calm. Nothing is amiss, but my ungrateful heart assures me that something has gone wrong.'[30]

Writing to Clive Bell in 1908, shortly after her arrival, Virginia was already voicing a restless yearning to be nearer the sea: 'Perhaps I shall enjoy an ecstasy upon the summit of the downs, from which Mrs Wall [her landlady] once, some 40 years ago, saw the sea. ... I am almost drowned in earth and antiquity here.'[31] Although Virginia too had managed to glimpse the sea, or rather the Bristol Channel, from the Mendips, to her mind Somerset was incomplete without Atlantic rollers:

Bristol Channel from the Quantocks

Hills really exist solely that you may have a wide view from them of the sea, the horizon, & one or two ships between. Then you get a kind of flow of life round you; you return content to the same fields again. But when you see nothing but land, stationary on all sides, you are conscious of being trapped, on a flat board.[32]

Near the end of Virginia's stay news eventually arrived of a cottage for rent on the Pembrokeshire coast and her letter to Lady Cecil expresses some of her pent up frustration: 'I have been drowsing here in the most ancient and most respectable of cities for a fortnight till I feel that I must get onto a cliff and scream at the Atlantic. Is it the Atlantic at South Wales?'[33] Two days later she left Wells to slumber on undisturbed and set out for the fishing village of Manorbier where she found the roar of the sea and the sound of gulls screeching overhead more conducive to writing.

Alfoxden House

In 1795 Coleridge too had left the Mendips in search of the Atlantic on a road that was to lead straight to Xanadu and 'The Rime of the Ancient Mariner.' On one of his great hikes in the company of Robert Southey he stopped in the village of Nether Stowey at the foot of the Quantock Hills. The following year, with the help of his friend Tom Poole, he found lodgings there in Lime Street for himself and his young family. The arrival of William and Dorothy Wordsworth two years later gave birth to the Romantic Movement and the great collaborative venture that produced the *Lyrical Ballads*. Furnished with her copy of the work and Dorothy's *Journal*, Virginia returned to Somerset in

August 1912 with Leonard Woolf for a brief literary honeymoon on the edge of the Quantocks. Her postcard to Lytton Strachey carried a picture of Alfoxden House, home of the Wordsworths, tucked away in the most beautiful wooded coomb less than a mile from where they had taken rooms in the Plough Inn at Holford. Here they hoped to retrace the footsteps of the young revolutionary poets across the hills but the weather was not kind: 'We've seen nothing of the Quantocks, except great shapes of mist, but we've walked to the top of them, and now we sit over a fire and read novels like tigers. ...'[34] she wrote to Janet Case before they left for more reliable weather on the continent.

developed a strong attachment to Ottoline Morrell, one that made him oblivious to the complexity of her romantic entanglements. During his recent holiday in Turkey with the Bells she had written about the sacred flame of friendship while resuming her affairs with the painter Henry Lamb and with Bertrand Russell. Brought low by a heavy cold she eventually sought sanctuary in Studland only to find her lodgings marooned in the

Clive Bell and Virginia, Studland Bay, 1910

middle of a cabbage field. Undeterred Lady Ottoline went for long, solitary walks beside the shore unaware that a relationship between Fry and Vanessa had begun to blossom in the intense heat. In Turkey Vanessa had become seriously ill following a miscarriage and her recovery was due largely to Fry who had nursed her back to health. On their return to England the affair continued at Studland where they both produced striking, reductive images of the bay. Lytton Strachey who had also arrived at Harbour View soon became irritated by fractious children – 'Julian is half-witted' – Clive's preposterous theories of art and life, Fry's romantic distractions and Virginia, observing all this with quiet detachment, but who 'rattles her accustomed rant.' Strachey was back in Dorset at the end of the year but this time in the company of Maynard Keynes and Rupert Brooke who had arranged a reading party in Lulworth. On this occasion it was Brooke who found his relationship with Ka Cox, the Fabian student he had met at Cambridge, rocked by her love for Henry Lamb. Brooke's rejection and his absurd attempt to implicate Strachey led indirectly to his alienation from the whole Bloomsbury group.

Virginia's last visit to Studland was in September 1923. She and Leonard stayed at The Knoll on the road to Sandbanks ferry as guests of Maynard Keynes who had rented the Duke of Hamilton's seaside retreat, complete with servants. Other guests included the poet George Rylands, the critic Raymond Mortimer, and Lydia Lopokova, the Russian dancer Keynes later married. Virginia's sense of place on this occasion was strictly hierarchical and the presence of Lydia, the daughter of a Petersburg hotel porter, enabled her to indulge her capacity for malicious gossip. In a letter to Jacques Raverat she reminded him that 'Lydia's habits, of course, are not ducal'[3] before recounting the incident of the Used Sanitary Towels deposited mysteriously in the fireplace. The unwelcome task of drawing the matter to Lydia's attention fell to the Duke's cook and caused an unholy row before the cook and the ballerina came to swear eternal friendship.

Lydia Lopokova and Duncan Grant, Studland, 1923

Woolbridge Manor beside the Frome

DORSET

One of the Turberville portraits that once adorned Woolbridge Manor

On one occasion Keynes took his house party on a tour of places made famous in Hardy's novels. They went first to Lulworth, or Lulwind Cove, as Hardy called it, where Sergeant Troy is swept out to sea between 'the pillars of Hercules to this miniature Mediterranean.'[3A] From here they drove to Warbarrow (not yet requisitioned by the military), climbed the cliff-top path and walked unheeded over the down towards Corfe Castle. Virginia was in reflective mood:

I thought of the year 1830, & how most of England then looked as this coast looked, bays with their sweep untenanted, only coastguards & gray cottages, & rowing boats making off to little ships ... The clear water was very moving to me, with the pale stones showing under it like jelly fish. Lulworth of course was all skittles, & men playing in a yard; & people parading in front of a wall which, like an Italian wall, encloses the headland.[4]

Before returning to Studland the party stopped at Woolbridge Manor by the banks of the Frome in Hardy's Vale of the Great Dairies. Here in the draughty, doom-laden ancestral home of the d'Urbervilles with its sinister family portraits, Angel Clare and his young bride spend the first night of their honeymoon and the past finally catches up with Tess. A few miles downstream is Bindon Abbey where, during the sleepwalking episode, Clare carries Tess across a narrow footbridge before laying her to rest in an open

Gatehouse to Bindon Abbey

grave. According to Hardy: 'Against the north wall was the empty stone coffin of an abbot, in which every tourist with a turn for grim humour was accustomed to stretch himself.'[5] The whole scene in what Virginia called 'this damp, romantic place'[6], given greater resonance by its new literary association, appealed to Lopokova's sense of the theatrical as she 'lay in her pink jacket with the white fur in a Bishop's tomb – a kind of shaped tank sunk in the earth ...'[7]

Three years later, in April 1926, the Woolfs were back in Dorset staying this time deep in Hardy country between Blandford and Shaftesbury. The contorted projections rising above Blackmore Vale are crowned by a succession of majestic hill forts that stand out like teeth in an old jaw. This is the great sinuous divide between two very different landscapes. In one direction the gentler, more secretive country of butter pastures, trout streams and luxuriant hedges spreads itself comfortably at the foot of the downs. Even the names of the villages strung along the margins of the vale that so delighted Virginia – Glanvilles Wootton, Okeford Fitzpaine and Hazelbury Bryan – still echo to the sound of Norman barons and the forest of Whitehart through which they hunted. Here in this predatory landscape is the village of Marnhull the childhood home of Hardy's 'pure woman', Tess d'Urberville; but for Virginia the vale, resolving itself into a series of Turneresque vistas, threatened nothing more sinister than a passing shower:

The abbot's coffin, Bindon Abbey

The Vale of Blackmore

... a vast air dome & the fields dropped to the bottom; the sun striking, there, there; a drench of rain falling, like a veil streaming from the sky, there & there; & the downs rising, very strongly scarped (if that is the word) so that they were ridged & ledged ...[8]

The Vale of Blackmore from Gold Hill, Shaftesbury

The village pump, Iwerne Minster

From her reading of *Jude the Obscure* Virginia had expected Shaftesbury – Hardy's Shaston – to be more dramatically perched above the Vale of Blackmore. Despite the gradient of Gold Hill and the sweeping view from the top of its famous cobbled street, the hill town remained for her 'so much lower & less commanding than my imagination.'[9] She was better pleased with Iwerne Minster, a few miles south on the main road to Blandford at the foot of Cranborne Chase, and their accommodation at the Talbot Inn where hot baths and log fires brightened a rather wet and windy few days. The village itself, ruled from the big house with a beneficent eye by James Ismay, a wealthy shipping magnate, was as neat and well-endowed as it could be. Writing to Vanessa in playful mood, Virginia described the place thus: '... rare flowers burst out of every cranny in every cottage; the villagers wear specially knitted red waistcoats, if male; if female, red cloaks. You might well eat off the street.'[10] The village institute, a recent gift from the lord of the manor, together with the primary school and the roadside inn where the Woolfs were staying, were all built in what the architectural historian, Nikolaus Pevsner, later described as 'a livery of loud red brick and prominent half timbered gables.'[11] This virulent style of 'stockbroker Tudor' was more reminiscent of the Home

ENGLISH HOURS

Counties than the West Country vernacular that impressed Virginia rather more. In this country of stone manor houses the most romantic for her was the ashlared façade of Stapleton House. Embedded in its parkland just a few miles south in the shadow of Hod Hill, it was once the home of Peter Beckford whose *Thoughts upon Hare and Fox-Hunting* (1789) became 'a model of stylish verve and practical information.'[12]

The Talbot Inn

Today Iwerne Minster, winner of the Dorset Best Kept Village competition on several occasions, is almost a parody of the place Virginia found so excessively clean. Claysmore, the High Victorian mansion from where Ismay, otherwise the second Baron Wolverton, ruled his subjects, is now a private school, but the whole place is forever preserved in aspic, dotted with reminders of the Baron's wealth and generousity like so many wayside shrines. Beneath a sturdy oak canopy the village pump is embossed with the initials of its donor while, opposite, the former bus shelter in local limestone is adorned, more in hope, with the winged figure of Mercury. The most impressive monument stands beside the main road, a beautifully engraved memorial to those killed in the Great War which, for its elegance and detail must be unique to the county. The lettered panels carry not only the name, rank and regiment of each victim but, most poignantly, the place and manner of their death – 'from the effects of German Gas poisoning' at the Somme etc. Virginia would have drawn some comfort from the Red Cross nurses listed among those killed in action, one who died of septicaemia, another of pneumonia at Reading War Hospital.

Iwerne Minster's Great War memorial

Above and beyond the chalk hills stretch away, a more ancient land of earthworks, sarsen stones and the remnants of Cranborne Chase from which Tess d'Urberville returns home 'a maid no more.' Virginia too, caught something of its sinister atmosphere: 'the stunted aboriginal forest trees, scattered, not grouped in cultivations; anemones, bluebells, violets, all pale, sprinkled about, without colour, livid, for the sun hardly shone.'[13] Sometime

Thomas Hardy, Florence and dog Wessex

before she had learnt to her pleasure that Hardy approved of *The Common Reader* (published the previous year) and the Woolfs intended to visit the great Dorset novelist before returning to Tavistock Square. In the event they allowed insufficient time for a trip to Dorchester but Virginia, who held Hardy in higher regard than any other living author, accepted an invitation to Max Gate in July. 'I never saw such a spruce lively old man, but nothing would induce him to talk about his books'[14] she wrote to Violet Dickinson. The novels, completed years before – *Jude the Obscure*, his last, was published in 1896 – he'd always regarded as hackwork and showed little interest in them now or indeed in any literature. This grand old man of English fiction was now far more interested in people and, between interruptions from his dog Wessex, talked with affection about Virginia's father who, as editor of *The Cornhill Magazine*, had commissioned Hardy's own favourite novel *Far From the Madding Crowd* (1886). After tea Hardy walked with his visitors to the road where they stood and admired the view out across the Dorset countryside: 'rolling, massive downs, crowned with little tree coronets ...'[15] before bidding them farewell. The timing of Virginia's visit may have been significant; she was emersed in *To The Lighthouse* (1927), recalling childhood memories of St Ives and Hardy provided a link with the past and, more importantly, with her father. Hardy died just two years later and Virginia, who attended the funeral in Westminster Abbey, wrote her own tribute shortly after in the *Times Literary Supplement* under the title 'Thomas Hardy's Novels.'

It was another ten years before Virginia returned to Dorset and then only briefly en route to Cornwall and a holiday with the Arnold-Forsters (see Chapt.I). With Leonard she chose to revisit the scene of her Dreadnought

Regency cottages, Marine Parade, Lyme Regis

Hoax but on this occasion Weymouth '... was sepulchral, like crawling under a grey umbrella; very cold and colourless. This was disappointing, as I rather think Weymouth is the most beautiful seaside town in Europe, combining the grace of Naples with the sobriety of George the Third.'[16] Following the king's much publicised dip in the ocean here in 1789 the place had been transformed into a fashionable resort. The Regency terraces strung out along the esplanade with names evocative of the period – Charlotte Row, Augusta Place and Brunswick Terrace – were certainly elegant, but as John Betjeman argued a decade after Virginia's visit, every sheltered bay with a resort is likened to Naples but 'is Naples called the Weymouth of Italy?'[17] His answer was a loud 'No', although his affection for the town remained undiminished.

From Weymouth the Woolfs moved quickly along the coast, deciding to put up for the night at Lyme Regis. The place was already familiar to Virginia from the family holiday taken here in April 1901 at Little Park, a charming thatched house owned by Leslie Stephen's friend, the poet Francis Palgrave. But on her return years later 'We were extravagant and stayed at the best hotel [either the Red Lion or the Three Cups, both in Broad Street], in which the very pots were seasoned with camphor'[18]. Here Virginia was just the latest in a long line of authors to pay homage at this most celebrated literary shrine. Mindful of the single dramatic incident in *Persuasion* with which Lyme is forever associated – Louisa Musgrove's celebrated tumble on the Cobb – she asked 'Why are all the West country towns precisely as they were in Jane Austens day?'[19] before heading west to the more rugged coastline of the Cornish peninsula.

'Granny's Teeth' on The Cobb

XI

SUSSEX

Look your last on all things lovely

Jack Hills, engaged to Virginia's half sister Stella Duckworth, underwent a minor operation in January 1897 that led to the postponement of their wedding and the choice of Bognor for his convalescence. It was decided that Virginia, who was vehemently opposed to the idea from the outset, should accompany the couple. She only acquiesced when Vanessa agreed to travel with her and the Stephen family eventually set off for what turned out to be a quite dreadful week at the seaside. Although the family had already been to Brighton on several occasions this was for Virginia, who had just decided to keep a diary, the beginning of a long, well documented affair with Sussex that lasted until her death in 1941.

Always a dismal prospect in mid-winter, Bognor at the turn of the century had seen better days. It was a product of the early 19th century seaside boom that had transformed the south coast and was strung out over the marshes of west Sussex. Positioned strategically between Bournemouth's wooded chines and Brighton's Royal Pavilion, the resort was destined to be the poor relation of them both despite its reputation as the model for Jane Austen's Sanditon. Bognor, epitome of the high Victorian resort, continued to sprawl along the coast, consuming everything in its path including the village where William Blake had composed 'Jerusalem' in 1800. As a respite from the grime of London's streets the place had been such a revelation to the young poet that he felt able to write 'Away to Felpham for heaven is there.' Having trudged along a deserted and windswept esplanade to their lodgings in Cotswold Crescent, Bognor must have seemed to Virginia a world away from Blake's 'dwelling for immortals.' She had come well prepared; among her reading material were several volumes of Scott and a novel by WE Norris entitled, *A Deplorable Affair*, that seemed more appropriate to the occasion.

As the weather deteriorated further even Leslie Stephen was forced to conclude: 'Never saw such an ugly country and such bad weather in my life.'[1] Aimless cycle rides along muddy tracks were followed by a disastrous outing to Arundel Castle. Having missed the train the visitors hired an open cart drawn at a snail's pace by an old nag through 'very flat, uninteresting country – great brown ploughed fields, and ditches and miserable wind blown trees –'[2]. When the horse refused to go any further its passengers walked the rest of the way only to find the castle closed for repairs. The suggestion, made

Cotswold Crescent, Bognor Regis, c.1890

without much conviction, that they might extend their holiday a little longer, was greeted with howls of protest from the Stephen sisters: 'Another week of drizzle in that muddy misty flat utterly stupid Bognor (the name suits it) would have driven me to the end of the pier and into the dirty yellow sea beneath –'[3]. Virginia may well have concurred with George V who, following a period of convalescence in 1929, is alleged to have retorted 'Bugger Bognor' when advised he was well enough for a return visit. Today the town still clings proudly to its 'Regis', acquired as a result of the royal visit, presumably in the belief that bad publicity is better than none at all.

Stella Duckworth and Jack Hills were married on April 10th 1897 and three days later Virginia, who had been reduced to a state of nervous exhaustion by the wedding preparations, went with her family for a two week holiday in

Brighton. Coming so soon after her Bognor experience she was decidedly unenthusiastic about another sojourn on the Sussex coast and the prospect of time spent with her Fisher relatives. Things started badly; the cycle ride planned on the first morning proving so disagreeable that Virginia and Vanessa left the others to struggle on and returned to the 'rather gruesome'[4] surroundings of No.9 St Aubyn's, Hove, where Virginia decided Macaulay's *History of England* was slightly more entertaining than negotiating a dust storm on the road to Shoreham. When the sun broke through on the following morning the Stephens joined the throng on the seafront providing Virginia with an opportunity to indulge her ingrained snobbery: '– a most disgusting spectacle, though rather amusing – all the third rate actresses turned out in gorgeous clothes – tremendous hats, powder and rouge; and dreadful young men to escort them –'[5].

One of the most popular local attractions was Devil's Dyke, an Iron Age hill fort and beauty spot six miles north west of Brighton. On Easter Monday Virginia and Vanessa, together with two of their Fisher cousins, braved the bank holiday crowds and took a short journey on the railway built to convey visitors to the top of the downs. Emerging from the guard's van with their bicycles the Stephen/Fisher clan tumbled down the steep chalk slopes and rode home in a downpour by way of Bramber and Shoreham. Despite the rain the trip to the Dyke was judged a success and several days later it was repeated

No. 9 St Aubyns, Hove

Great West Pier, Brighton, c1900

but the long, exhilarating descent into Brighton proved a rather bruising experience: 'All the winds that have had a place in this diary, must yield ignominiously to the wind which met us now – Several times I was blown into hedges, and the bicycles behaved in a most drunk way –'[6]. Undeterred by their previous visit the two sisters set out for Arundel once more in rather better weather, determined to gain entry. The keep was open but 'The castle is all being hideously rebuilt'[7] – an unconvincing reconstruction by C A Buckler in a pastiche of the medieval building.

On New Year's day 1911 Virginia was writing to Ottoline Morrell: 'Here I am sitting over an inn fire, and listening to the creaking of an enormous sign, painted with your family arms.'[8] She had come with her brother to the Pelham Arms in Lewes, while Vanessa spent Christmas in Wiltshire with the Bells, and seemed determined their visit should not go unnoticed. 'Adrians hair flows like a crazy poets'[9] from beneath a strawberry roan coloured hat purchased for the occasion, while Virginia took to the downs in a flowing purple cape thrown over her red dress, flitting from mound to mound like an emperor butterfly. Bloomsbury had arrived in Sussex, to the consternation of its more conservative locals and the mild amusement of others.

The previous year Virginia had been admitted to a private nursing home in Twickenham suffering from nervous exhaustion. The weeks here, followed by a walking holiday in Cornwall and a recuperative trip to Dorset (see Chapt. X) appeared to have revived her spirits, but her health was still fragile and once back in Fitzroy Square the demands of London life threatened to plunge her once more into madness. As an antidote she was persuaded to look for a country retreat within reach of the capital and had descended on Sussex armed with a selection of OS maps and local guide books. With its open chalk hills, its wide river valleys and the coast all easily accessible from London by train, this part of southern England had much to offer and Virginia soon declared herself 'violently in favour of a country life.'[10]

Days later while in Lewes she discovered the village of Firle just a few miles distant. Tucked away off the main road at the foot of the downs, Firle Place had been the ancestral home of the Gage family for the last 500 years and the village seemed to satisfy Virginia's need for stability and seclusion nurtured by a landscape of sublime beauty. The nearest station was only a mile away at Glynde and, charmed by what she had seen, Virginia decided to rent a property from the estate. Ironically the only place available was not the

The 'creaking sign', Lewes High Street

country cottage she had planned but a recently completed Edwardian semi. As she admitted to Molly MacCarthy, the writer and wife of Bloomsberry Desmond MacCarthy: 'The villa is inconceivably ugly, done up in patches of post-impressionist colour'[11], a reference to Roger Fry's recently organised exhibition at the New Grafton Gallery. Tall, heavily gabled and Tudoresque with false beams and hung tiles it remains a clumsy indiscretion rising above the rows of neat estate cottages in the village street. Virginia tried to console herself by renaming it Little Talland in memory of the Cornish house where, as a child, she had enjoyed so many family holidays. She also argued, with less conviction, that once inside such an eyesore it could be conveniently forgotten.

Firle Place

In the coming weeks Virginia was often down at Firle making arrangements which included 'sitting naked before the Vicars gardener'[12] until her housekeeper managed to put up some heavy curtains. Soon she felt able to announce that Little Talland was ready to receive guests. Among the first to arrive was Ka Cox who came 'striding along the road ... with a knapsack on her back, a row of red beads, and daisies stuck in her coat'[13] full of Neo-Pagan entanglements that she unravelled at length in Firle park. Having rejected Walter Lamb's offer of marriage, Virginia felt able to invite Mr Woolf, recently returned from Ceylon, for his first weekend at her 'cottage in the Sussex downs.'[14] Thrown into confusion by his prompt acceptance she wrote again briefly to confess that it was no more than 'a hideous suburban villa'.[15]

Little Talland (left) 'inconcievably ugly'

Between entertaining friends Virginia embraced the solitary life and soon slipped into a daily routine that was to serve her well in Sussex. Mornings were always reserved for writing, for her novel *Melymbrosia* and for reviews, while the evenings were for reading. After lunch each new walk took her deeper into a countryside bursting with life. Returning home from one such adventure, having just clambered out of a muddy ditch, she met Lord Gage in the village with a 'face like a dead hares'[16] hobbling along on the vicar's arm to inspect the ancestral tombs. Two years later the 5th Viscount was dead and the public memorial erected in his honour opposite Little Talland as a parish Reading Room, was the kind of philanthropic gesture likely to have met with the young novelist's approval.

Three miles north of Firle, approached down a track through meadows drained by the Glynde Reach, stands a 16th century brick tower. Lovingly restored by the Landmark Trust the building has an illustrious pedigree which, according to the Trust's handbook 'it wears with the lonely and battered dignity of a nobleman fallen on hard times.' Once the main seat of the Pelhams, Laughton Place was remodelled on a grand scale in 1543 around

Laughton Tower

a moated courtyard; and when Virginia first discovered it in April 1911 it still resembled 'a mediaeval castle [ ] in the marsh'[17]. Years later during her affair with Vita Sackville-West, Virginia went with her lover from Monks House to see this most romantic of ruins. Mindful of Vita's grand ancestral pile at Knole and seduced by the heat of a late summer's afternoon she devised extravagant plans to buy Laughton but to Leonard's relief her enthusiasm quickly evaporated on a return visit when the accommodation proved to be 'unspeakably dreary'[18].

As the months went by the tenant of Little Talland became more dissatisfied with her cramped accommodation and used it rather as a base from which to look for something larger and more attractive. Having already become a frequent visitor at 29 Fitzroy Square, Leonard Woolf was unable to honour Virginia's invitation to Sussex until the September of 1911. As it transpired, the weekend became hugely significant for them both. Leonard's feelings for Virginia became increasingly bound up in his emotional response to the landscape:

It was still the unending summer of that marvellous year, and it seemed as if the clouds would never again darken the sky as we sat reading in Firle Park or walked over the downs. This was the first time that I had seen the South Downs as it were from the inside and felt the beauty of the gentle white curves of the fields between the great green curves of their hollows.[19]

Looking west to Firle Beacon

One of Virginia's favourite walks took her and Leonard out of the village along a track opposite the church and up the steep north slope of the chalk scarp. At the top the couple headed west along the ridge before descending into a hidden valley let into the side of Itford Hill. Here they stumbled upon 'an extraordinarily romantic-looking house,'[20] a house 'dropped beneath the Downs'[21] and hemmed in by a thick belt of trees. Apart from a shepherd's cottage it stood quite alone on the edge of the Ouse valley facing west with a long view to Rodmell and the ripple of hills beyond. Asheham, built for a local solicitor in the 1820s, was a charming Regency house, its plain limewash façade embellished by a set of tall Gothick windows and flanked by two low pedimented wings. It was light, spacious and serene with French windows opening on to the terrace and bore more than a passing resemblance to Talland House in Cornwall. In winter, with the whole valley flooded, the spire of Rodmell church became a point of reference that beckoned on the far side, in the manner of Godrevy lighthouse.

Asheham House, oil on canvas, Vanessa Bell, 1912

Asheham stood empty and inviting. Virginia and Leonard were both struck by the strength of its personality; 'romantic, gentle, melancholy, lovely.'[22] With the excitement of their discovery still fresh in her mind Virginia moved quickly to secure a five year lease on the property which she had agreed to share with Vanessa. The first of many Bloomsbury house parties, arranged hastily in February 1912, was memorable for the bleakness of the occasion and seemed to foreshadow the difficulties that lay ahead.

It was the coldest day for 40 years, all the pipes were frozen; the birds were starving against the window panes; some had got in, and sat by the fire; the bottom fell out of the grates; suddenly Marjorie [Strachey], who was reading Racine, stopped dead and said "I have got chicken pox."[23]

Virginia was less sure about her feelings for Leonard. She had grown to enjoy his company and looked forward to their meetings but it was several months after his first proposal that she agreed to marry him, the ceremony taking place in August 1912 at St Pancras registry office. Her initial indecision coupled with the expectations of married life and the completion of her first novel conspired to bring about another breakdown. This time it lasted through much of the following year and returned as a more violent form of madness in 1915. During prolonged periods of convalescence and throughout her time at Asheham Virginia drew strength from the simple pleasures of country living; harvesting the mushrooms that grew in profusion on the slopes behind the house or scouring the hedgerows for blackberries. She attended cookery classes, perfected the art of bread making and pickled their crop of walnuts. Between helping to care for Virginia and his own writing Leonard tackled the 'small, dishevelled walled garden'[24] with great enthusiasm, pruned the fruit trees, planted the flower beds and laid a network of cobble paths.

Asheham House, 1991, shortly before demolition

At Asheham the Woolfs slipped easily into the uneventful routine of rural life. In the drawing room 'The window-panes reflected apples, reflected roses; all the leaves were green in the glass.'[25] Days melted into each other and as the house became submerged in lush vegetation Virginia felt increasingly '[i]ts very like living at the bottom of the sea being here – one sometimes hears rumours of what is going on overhead.'[26] Writing to Ottoline Morrell at the end of the war she refers again to the soporific effect of life at Asheham: 'The time passes, with proper nights and days, I suppose, but one seems to float through them in a disembodied kind of way here.'[27] The deep silence of the house, disturbed only by the sound of the wind in the chimney or rats in the cellar together with this distorted sense of time, gave Virginia the idea for 'A Haunted House':

In the story the wind rages through the trees, '[m]oonbeams splash and spill wildly in the rain,'[28] but inside all is calm. The candle burns still as the ghostly couple, returning to their old home, pass from room to room in search of the treasure they left behind there in 'the pulse of the house.'[29] The story was not published until 1921 but, as Hermione Lee suggests in her biography of Woolf (1996), it may also have its origins in a wartime article by Virginia that appeared in *The Times*. In 'Heard on the Downs: The Genesis of Myth' (1916) the oral tradition of 'ghostly riders and unhappy ladies forever seeking their lost treasure'[30] that still lingered in the more remote downland communities is given new life by the dull thud of distant gunfire, a sound which she likens to the beating of gigantic carpets:

Leonard Woolf (left) and Adrian Stephen at Asheham

All walks on the Downs this summer are accompanied by this sinister sound of far-off beating, which is sometimes as faint as the ghost of an echo, and sometimes rises almost from the next fold of grey land.[31]

A South Downs shepherd

Strange noises caught in the smooth downland hollows had always been given lurid shape by itinerant story tellers but their tales were now compounded by the spectre of war 'hovering on the borderland of belief and scepticism.'[32] Addled farm eggs, the recent spell of cloudy weather and other seasonal abnormalities were all credited to shock waves emanating from the heavy artillery exchanges on the western front. The conflict continued to impinge on life at Asheham in more tangible ways throughout the summer of 1917. Guests were requested to bring their own provisions and Nelly, who had come with the Woolfs from Richmond and who found the house damp and depressing, had run terrified into the wood at the sight of a Zeppelin hovering overhead. Virginia's diary entry for September 5th in which commonplace observations of the natural world are interwoven with images of war, is typical:

> I saw a clouded yellow on the top – a very deep yellow the first for a long time. Clouds brewed over the sea, & it began to rain at tea; then great thunderclaps, & lightning. Difficult to distinguish thunder from guns. German prisoners walked across the field.[33]

The natural world continued to provide Virginia with a fund of anecdotes that give her correspondence the authentic flavour of country life. After a visit to Garsington she complained to Ottoline Morrell that they were 'suffering from a plague of small frogs and black beetles, who come in through the windows.'[34] To Dora Carrington she recounted the occasion when '[a] swarm of bees conglobulated suddenly over our heads on the terrace – in an ecstasy of lust.'[35] Clearly disturbed by the cacophonous surge of procreation each spring she wrote in exasperation to Lytton Strachey:

> Its all very well to come to the country in order to write, but the animals are carrying on so frantically and indecently that I can't hear myself speak. Lambs, thrushes, ewes, rooks – their conduct is too distracting. I find that scarcely anything but impassioned meditation stands up against it, and the passion tends to run much in a groove.[36]

Domestic pets proved equally distracting. Virginia's unruly dogs were allowed to rampage over the hills during the lambing season, an act of gross irresponsibility that drew a stern rebuke from their local gamekeeper, and shortly after she had to inform Leonard that 'Shot crashed through the drawing room window this morning'[37]. Her initial enthusiasm for riding was tempered by a series of falls that left her bruised and shaken, an experience she seemed anxious to share with guests. Inviting Molly MacCarthy for the weekend she added mischievously: 'You will find [E M] Forster here, but he is going to be put on the brood mare, who has become very fresh, so we shan't see much of him.'[38] Country walks with house guests could occasionally prove rather tiresome. When Roger Fry's friend, the poet Bob Trevelyan, had been to stay Virginia confessed to Saxon Sydney-Turner 'you can imagine what it was like walking on the top of the Downs in a high wind, with him talking quite incessantly about poetry religion etc. beside one. At last about 11 o'clock at night, he stopped and said he really didn't know what he was talking about.'[39] Presumably by this time they were either completely lost or safely back at Asheham.

Charleston today

For Virginia the most significant effect of the war was Vanessa's decision to move to Charleston. In 1916 she had left Asheham to spend the summer in Suffolk with Duncan Grant and David Garnett (see Chapt.VII) leaving

Virginia to relay the news to Ka Cox: 'So you see, Bloomsbury is vanished like the morning mist.'[40] As conscientious objectors Grant and Garnett eventually gained exemption from military service on the condition that they find employment as farm labourers and, much to Virginia's relief, this prompted a swift return to Sussex. Life together at Asheham had not been

Janet Case, Virginia and Vanessa in Firle Park, 1911

without its practical difficulties, difficulties that arose primarily over the question of servants, but Virginia was anxious to have her sister nearby. She wrote enthusiastically about the farmhouse Leonard had discovered beyond Firle and it appeared to fulfil Vanessa's immediate requirements. Grant and Garnett could work on the estate, it was a convenient distance from Asheham and she became excited by its artistic possibilities; the relationship of farm buildings to the pond, the walled garden and the soft contours of the hills behind. Once Vanessa was installed, Virginia was soon striding over these same hills to share a picnic with her sister on Firle Beacon or cycling through the park in time for tea. Occasionally she stayed overnight and there, removed from the serious business of writing, the sounds of spring time that two months earlier had proved so distracting, soothed her to sleep:

Last night at Charleston I lay with my window open listening to a nightingale, which beginning in the distance came very near the garden. Fishes splashed in the pond. May in England is all they say – so teeming, amorous, & creative.[41]

From the bugging expeditions of her childhood, Virginia had become a competent naturalist and the first few months of the diary she resumed in August 1917 are filled with brief observations made on her walks to Firle or on mushrooming expeditions across the river at Southease and up to Telscombe. Here the short, springy downland turf was studded with wild flowers; with ladies bedstraw, round-headed campion, thyme and field gentian. Peacock butterflies and silver washed fritillaries danced in the warm air while 'innumerable blues [were] feeding on dung.'[42] Late summer gales had brought down trees and flattened the corn so that '[s]wallows & leaves whirling about look much the same.'[43] These nature notes – they hardly qualify as sketches of country life – are quite devoid of sentimentality. Horse-drawn mowing machines at work in the fields and thistledown drifting in the air are common enough sights recorded in the same perfunctory manner and balanced by the realities of village life:

Firle post office where Virginia and Vanessa often met for a picnic in the park

– Went to post at Southease ... Saw wooden pews put into traction engine at Rodmell Church; a man without a hand, a hook instead. Met Mrs Attfield with dead chicken in a parcel, found dead in the nettles, head wrung off, perhaps by a person.[44]

In September 1918 the weather and the occasion conspired to produce one of those rare transcendent moments that had inspired the mysticism of Richard Jefferies' autobiographical *The Story of My Heart* (1894) and were to distinguish Llewelyn Powys' collection of essays *Earth Memories* (1934), conceived on his own patch of Dorset downland. For Virginia on this particular day:

> ... the weather has been so tremendously generous, giving us after a veil of morning mist, such an endowment of sun & such clouds of alabaster firmly laid against the blue, ... I remember lying on the side of a hollow, waiting for L. to come & mushroom, & seeing a red hare loping up the side & thinking suddenly "This is Earth Life". I seemed to see how earthy it all was, & I myself an evolved kind of hare; as if a moon-visitor saw me.[45]

Telscombe down

Throughout the seven years Virginia and Leonard were at Asheham she spent long periods in bed recovering from a series of breakdowns including at least one attempted suicide. There can be little doubt that in less peaceful surroundings and without the watchful eye of her husband she would not have survived, but here, encouraged by the favourable reviews that greeted the publication of her first novel in 1915, Virginia found the strength to complete *Night and Day* (1919). At the end of the war the Woolfs were informed that the house would be needed for a second farm bailiff and, just a couple of months before their departure, Virginia acknowledged her debt to the place on a perfect June day.

I dozed & drowsed & seemed to feel the sun in my brain sending all my thoughts to seek repose in the shadow. I write there at an open window looking onto the field; & the field was gilt with buttercups; the sheep were tempting in their indolence; ... Our ship rode so steady that one came to disbelieve in motion or the possibility of change; we appeared wedged in the blue. Perhaps one day there was a cloud; but no harbourage was offered it, & congregation of clouds was impossible. The loveliness of Asheham once again brimmed the cup & overflowed.[46]

Virginia drew great comfort from the landscape around Asheham and any regrets about leaving the house were dispelled by their decision to remain in the Ouse valley – 'To give up every foothold in that region seemed unthinkable.'[47] The Woolfs were soon caught up in the pleasures of house hunting and considered several possibilities before alighting on Monks House. Leonard scoured the countryside and came back with news of a 'large, stuffy, ill lit, slightly mouldy & decayed mansion'[48] in Denton. They went to Iford 'a thickly set little village on the plain'[49] between Rodmell and Lewes to look at a farmhouse that was too genteel – 'We have grown out of gentlemen's houses'[50] – and turned their attention once more to Itford Manor

Itford Manor

just a mile south of Asheham, soon to be vacated by the farm bailiff, but it was no longer available. They even flirted with the idea of building their own house, of securing a cottage in Firle and moving to Cornwall (see Chapt. I), before Virginia discovered the kind of property that all writers are meant to inhabit – a converted windmill in the shadow of Lewes castle with glorious views out over the town and the wooded vale towards Ashdown Forest:

> Off I went, up Pipes Passage, under the clock, & saw rising at the top of the sloping path a singular shaped roof, rising into a point, & spreading out in a circular petticoat all round it.[51]

The Round House

The Round House, created from the butt end of a brick and flint corn mill and crowned by an octagonal slate roof, stood bathed in sunlight; it was for sale, the asking price of £300 seemed reasonable and, charmed by what she had seen, Virginia decided to make an offer without consulting her husband. A few days later as they walked up from the station to inspect their new home Leonard caught sight of a placard announcing the sale of a property in

Rodmell with an acre of land. Suddenly the Round House seemed less attractive; the day was overcast, the rooms were cramped, the garden tiny and the countryside a distant prospect. It had been, as Virginia admitted, a reckless purchase and she agreed to cycle over to Rodmell the following day. Determined to remain level-headed – 'Monks are nothing out of the way'[52] – she arrived armed with 'prudent objections'[53] but commonsense prevailed:

> There is little ceremony or precision at Monks House. It is an unpretending house, long & low, a house of many doors; on one side fronting the street of Rodmell, & wood boarded on that side, though the street of Rodmell is at our end little more than a cart track running out on to the flat of the water meadows.[54]

Monks House, Rodmell

This diary extract for July 3rd 1919 with its reference to 'our end' was written two days after the auction. Once outside any misgivings Virginia may have had about the house 'were forced to yield to a profound pleasure'[55] at the garden with its orchard, its lawn and well-stocked vegetable plot running beside the wall of St Peter's churchyard. Leonard, too, was excited by the garden while Virginia began to appreciate the possibilities of its setting with 'the grey extinguisher of the church steeple pointing my boundary.'[56] The Telscombe downs lay behind the village and to the north were sweeping views across the Ouse flood plain to Mount Caburn; while the wooded slopes of Asheham Hill rose just beyond the river. These old, familiar landmarks appeared as new, the landscape became rearranged and Virginia knew she could live here within the confines of the hills she had grown to love. The Woolfs decided to put the Round House back on the market and two days later found themselves seated in the White Hart in Lewes. A few nervous minutes elapsed before they emerged into the High Street having bought Monks House for £700.

Virginia's writing hut, rebuilt by the National Trust

The building is said to date from the 15th or 16th century; if the latter then near enough to the Dissolution to question the tradition that it was once used as a retreat by the monks of Lewes Priory. There is documentary evidence that the c12 village church was once owned by the Cluniac foundation and, according to Nikolaus Pevsner, an ornamental basalt pillar was probably removed from the priory lavatorium. The proximity of St Peter's may help explain the name Monks House, or it may refer to an earlier building on the site. Virginia and Leonard, who would have liked to believe the story, remained sceptical but never felt strongly enough to re-christen their new home.

The spartan comforts of Monks House were, however, decidedly monastic, even by Bloomsbury standards. The floors were damp, the low beamed rooms dark and cold. Like most country cottages at that time it had no electricity or bathroom and the earth closet was approached with some trepidation through a tangle of laurel bushes. It was only later, following the success of Virginia's novels, that the Woolfs were able to put much of this right, but in the early years she often considered moving elsewhere in Sussex. Once Virginia had finished redecorating the house – she favoured arsenic green for the living room – the walls hung with Bloomsbury pictures and lined with books, she began to feel more at home and conceded that the place 'improves, after the fashion of a mongrel who wins your heart.'[57] The house had been owned by a 19th century family of millers and the three

One of three Glazebrook portraits

charming Glazebrook portraits purchased by the Woolfs provided a link with the village while the Omega furniture, much of it decorated by Vanessa and Duncan Grant was a reminder of London's artistic life to which they returned each winter. Mr Dedman, the admirably named village sexton, was another link with Rodmell society. He was employed as the Woolf's gardener and thereby achieved the distinction of working on both sides of the churchyard wall while his wife became the family cook and a source of local gossip that was not always welcome.

Virginia's bedroom, Monks House, 1930

For many years Virginia used an old apple store in the walled garden as her study in which she was often assailed by pleasurable distractions: 'temptation whispers from the window all the time.'[58] The well-stocked garden, the flowers from Leonard's greenhouses and the prospect of new walks each day soon compensated for the loss of Asheham's 'flawless beauty'[59].

Then theres Asheham hill smoke misted; the windows of the long train spots of sun; the smoke lying back on the carriages like a rabbits lop ears. The chalk quarry glows pink; & my water meadows lush as June, until you see that the grass is short, & rough as a dogfishes back .... Every day or nearly I've walked towards a different point & come back with a string of these matchings & marvels ...
... Yesterday I explored towards the house with the white chimneys, [Sutton House, upstream at Iford], finding a grass drive all the way; brooks struck off to the right blue as if with sea water. From one a snipe rose zigzagging across & across, flurried & swift. As I advanced the peewits rose in clouds ...[60]

This extract from Virginia's diary is from January 7th 1920, less than a year after the Woolfs' move. Over the next two decades her detailed account of Bloomsbury gossip, literary preoccupations, the problem of servants and the demands of the Hogarth Press is underpinned by passages of precise observation that record her delight in the changing year and the profound silence of Rodmell wrapped in a landscape of unsurpassed beauty:

ENGLISH HOURS

By opening the garden door I enlarge our garden so far as Mount Caburn. There I walk in the sunset; when the village climbing the hill has a solemn sheltering look [,] pathetic, somehow, emblematic, anyhow very peaceful & human, as if people sought each others company at night, & lived trustfully beneath the hills.'[61]

Rodmell church with Mount Caburn beyond

– days when the wind blew from every quarter at the top of its voice, & great spurts of rain came with it, & hail spat in our fire, & the lawn was strewn with little branches, & there were fiery sunsets over the downs, & one evening of the curled feathers that are so intense ...[62]

(... the village standing out to sea in the June night, houses seeming ships, the marsh a fiery foam) & the immense comfort of lying there lapped in peace.[63]

Back from a good weekend at Rodmell – a week end of no talking, sinking at once into deep safe book reading; & then sleep: clear transparent; with the may tree like a breaking wave outside; & all the garden green tunnels, mounds of green: & then to wake into the hot still day ...[64]

Merely scribbling here, over a log fire, on a cold but bright Easter morning; sudden shafts of sun, a scatter of snow on the hills early; sudden storms, ink black, octopus pouring, coming up; & the rooks fidgeting & pecking in the elm trees. As for the beauty ... too much for one pair of eyes.[65]

Throughout her time in Sussex Virginia was fiercely protective towards her adopted landscape. She became increasingly disturbed by the way the modern world encroached upon and threatened to violate the sanctity of Rodmell so essential to both her creativity and her sanity. In the 1920s Rodmell was a dying village as its young people drifted to the towns in search of work but Virginia found the influx of wealthy Londoners particularly distasteful, not least because she too was part of that same trend – the garage at Monks House had once been the village forge. Each year the editor of the *London Mercury* brought The Invalids, an ad hoc team of literary friends that included Siegfried Sassoon, to challenge the village cricket team in the meadows

Mount Caburn, 1935, watercolour, Eric Ravilious

alongside Monks House. After their departure Virginia complained: 'Somehow that the downs should be seen by cultivated eyes, self conscious eyes, spoils them to me.'[66] In March 1921 she attended a ghastly tea party at the rectory, a gathering of local literati and metropolitan exiles with whom she had no wish to be associated. Among those present was the poet Richard Burton who, with his wife, were to take Charnes Cottage next door to Monks House. The prospect filled Virginia with horror, she wrote in exasperation 'Rodmell is a colony for Georgian poets ...'[67]

Her attitude to James Allison, Rodmell's chief landowner, was slightly more conciliatory. She preferred farmers of local stock, 'muddy & ruddy & obsolete,'[68] but Allison, an Australian newspaper editor, was already a leading member of village society and a conscientious landlord who repaired his cottages, maintained his hedges and provided teas in his barn each summer. Unfortunately, Allison's land extended right to the boundary of Monks House and soon after their arrival the Woolfs were dismayed to learn that he had sold the adjoining field to a London solicitor as a building plot. The view out across the Ouse 'flats' would be ruined and the Woolfs' first reaction was to look elsewhere – a property near Arundel or a new house of their own. Mercifully the land was not developed and, after several attempts, they managed to buy the field in 1928 and allay Virginia's fears. But ownership itself is no absolute guarantee as the Woolfs discovered ten years later when they had to fight the Rural District Council's attempt to compulsorily acquire the same meadow for a sewage pumping station.

Edwardian crowds, Brighton seafront

Long after her Fisher relatives had ceased to contaminate the place Virginia became a regular visitor to Brighton but her attitude to this most regal of resorts remained ambivalent. On a trip with Leonard in October 1915, paid for out of proceeds from *The Voyage Out*, Virginia was more indulgent: '... wandering into back streets full of most improper little shops, and past the great bow windows, where the old ladies and their pets were sunning themselves'[69] – no whiff of prejudice or cheap perfume on this occasion. Writing to Violet Dickinson in 1924, she felt moved to declare: 'It is the most beautiful town in the whole world'[70], but never quite managed to reconcile the splendour of its Regency architecture with the spivs and tarts who loitered along the sea front or the 'shell encrusted old women, rouged, decked, cadaverous ...'[71] , who frequented the town's many tea shops. Towards the end of her life she had begun to grow weary of Brighton. One of her last diary entries – for February 26th 1941 – includes an image of voracious consumption which is both confirmation that the spectre of Aunt Mary Fisher still cast a long shadow and a reminder of the vulgar red brick villas crawling over her beloved downs:

Peacehaven

A fat, smart woman, in red hunting cap, pearls, check shirt, consuming rich cakes. Her shabby dependant was also stuffing. ... Something scented, shoddy, parasitic about them. ... Where does the money come to feed these fat white slugs? Brighton a love corner for slugs. The powdered the pampered the mildly improper.[72]

ENGLISH HOURS

All through the 1930s Virginia had seen her precious countryside shrink still further as the 'blasphemy of Peacehaven'[73] and Newhaven, all 'spot & rash & pimple & blister'[74] spread their tentacles unchecked towards the crest of the downs: 'one runs off the edge of the lovely into hideousness too soon.'[75] Peacehaven, or New Anzac-on-Sea, as it was first called, had been laid out on a grid of streets to commemorate the Antipodean expeditionary force but to Virginia it was just part of the suburban sprawl that threatened the smooth line of her sublime downs. This most dreadful rash of bungalow development imposed on the cliff top between Brighton and Newhaven was often cited in the debate then raging about the destruction of the English countryside; a debate that led eventually to the 1947 Town and Country Planning Act, the acquisition of the Seven Sisters by the National Trust and, after a lengthy campaign, the declaration of the South Downs as a National Park in 2009.

The Seven Sisters, saved by the Enterprise Neptune campaign

Many of Virginia's contemporaries watched in horror as the tide of speculative building engulfed large swathes of the south coast. In *Howards End* (1910) the view from Purbeck is already tainted by Bournemouth's stockbroker villas (see Chapt. X) and, brought up on the edge of Poole harbour, the Dorset novelist Mary Butts witnessed with a sense of rising panic the same restless 'maggot-knot of dwellings'[75A] edge its way through the woods and sweep away her childhood home. Away to the south the Purbeck Hills became a sacred land and the setting for several of Butts' novels including *Ashe of Rings* (1925). Although the struggle between aesthetic aspiration and an increasingly ugly world was a theme with which Virginia could identify, her literary judgement remained unmoved by such arguments. Butts' 'indecent book, about the Greeks and the Downs'[76] was summarily rejected by the Hogarth Press.

Angelica Garnett, Vanessa and Clive Bell, Virginia and Maynard Keynes outside the writing hut, Monks House, 1935

More immediately the pleasure of life at Monks House was constantly undermined by the threat of development and Virginia's diary becomes, incidentally, a chronicle of desecration. One particularly offensive red brick villa, dubbed 'Hancock's Horror,' appeared on Mill Hill above Rodmell in 1930, built for an unsuccessful Labour candidate. The following year Virginia noted 'the pink slate abortion on the Telscombe horizon'[77] that was Goat Farm and in 1937 another newspaper editor, JW Drawbell, raised another blot on the landscape further up Mill Lane. Rumours that Place Farm had been bought up for development simply confirmed her vision of a countryside 'crusted over with villas'[78].

The choice of Monks House by two people who valued seclusion so highly was in some ways curious. Its position on the edge of the meadows and the exciting possibilities of the garden were sufficient to overcome any initial reservations Virginia may have had about the uncomfortable proximity of both the church and the village school. In her short story 'In the Orchard' the sound of the children reciting their tables, the 'pensive and lugubrious note'[79] of the church organ and the squeak of its weathervane all drift unobtrusively on the breeze. Here they mingle with the thoughts of a woman dozing beneath the apple trees but to Virginia, at work in her garden studio, the church bells 'thudded, intermittent, sullen, didactic,'[80] and the noise of children at play in the meadow soon became a source of irritation. Only at the end of their first full summer in the village could she afford to be more generous:

> Even the schoolchildren's voices, if one thinks of them as swifts & martins skirling round the eaves, exhilarate instead of annoying. We now give them apples, rejecting their pence, & requiring in return that they shall respect the orchard ...
>
> One of the charms of Rodmell is the human life: everyone does the same thing at the same hour; when the old vicar performs erratically on the bells, after churching the women, everybody hears him, & knows what he's up to. Everyone is in his, or their garden; lamps are lit, but people like the last daylight ... What I mean is that we are a community.[81]

Virginia in the garden at Monks House, 1931

This rather romantic notion of village life, bathed in the warm glow of a summer evening, is more typical of the newcomer in search of identity, but Virginia's attitude to Rodmell society was normally less enthusiastic. Her sketch of Mrs Grey, whom the Woolfs visited with a gift of plums, is decidedly unsentimental; this unfortunate woman lived alone, suffered from dropsy and longed for death: 'She is shrunk, & sits on a hard chair in the corner, the door open. She twitches & trembles. Has the wild expressionless stare of the old. L. liked her despair ...'[82]. Virginia's portrait of the elderly and negligent Rev'd. Hawkesford, Rodmell's vicar since 1896, is equally uncharitable. Written the year before his death in 1928 it seems to confirm her disdain for the established church:

He is an old decaying man, run to seed ... wearing black wool mittens. ... To look at, he is like some aged bird; ... his beard is like an unweeded garden. ... He smokes endless cigarettes, & his fingers are not very clean. Talking of his well, he said "It would be a different thing if one wanted baths"– [83]

Virginia recalled how in his dotage the vicar did little but regale those willing to listen with tales of the more prominent local residents or, leaning over the stile, discuss Aladdin lamps with the neighbouring rector of Iford. Never once was he heard to discuss his vocation. In 'Miss Pryme,' one of several village stories set in Rodmell, there are no candles on Mr Pember's altar, the font leaks and the unkempt vicar of this 'corrupt village'[84] is caught by Rusham's (Rodmell's) most recent London exile 'slipping out in the middle of the service and smoking a cigarette in the graveyard.'[85]

In another entry from her 1927 diary entitled 'A Graveyard Scene,' Virginia describes the digging of a grave for the son of Henry Malthouse, the landlord of the Abergavenny Arms. This young sailor had died of consumption and, while her husband worked, the sexton's wife, Mrs Avery, 'immensely flat & florid, was sprawling on the edge of the grave, with her small children playing about.'[86] They were enjoying a picnic, a scene which suggested to Virginia a rather sentimental picture by Millais and one which found its way into the third tableau of her story 'Three Pictures'. By this process Virginia was able to transform the incidents of daily life into a more palatable version of Rodmell. 'The Widow and the Parrot,' subtitled ' A True Story', is a comic tale based on a fragment of village lore and the ruins of a cottage gutted by fire. In it the local family name of Gage is assumed by an elderly Yorkshire widow who arrives in Rodmell to reclaim her inheritance. Farmer Stacey, the Rev'd. Hawkesford, and a certain Leonard Woolf, lately of Asheham House, all make brief appearances and even the buckets used to dowse the flames are filled from the well at Monks House.

Cement Works No 2,
(the Alpha works)
Eric Ravilious, c.1934

Early in 1932 Virginia lamented the destruction of another view of the downs by the construction of the Alpha cement works: 'vast elephant grey sheds at Asheham, but I intend to see them as Greek temples'[87]. This is how she coped with the worst excesses of the material world – by trying to ignore them or by transforming them into something dignified. Despite the villas and rumours of industrial units all the way along the valley between Newhaven and Lewes, the temptation to move away was always offset by the deeply ingrained rhythm of life at Monks House and her ability to 'fasten on a beautiful day, as a bee fixes itself on a sunflower. It feeds me, rests me, satisfies me, as nothing else does –'[88]

Since their arrival in Sussex the Woolfs and the Bells had been in the habit of retreating to the metropolitan comforts of Bloomsbury each winter but with the onset of war they decided it would be marginally safer to remain in the country. The destruction soon after of the Woolfs' old home in Tavistock Square and the flat they had recently acquired in Mecklenburgh Square demonstrated most graphically the wisdom of this decision. At the same time Virginia's bouts of influenza throughout January and February 1940 combined with a prolonged period of sub-zero temperatures to test her resolve. Compounded by the privations of rationing and the blackout, the

SUSSEX

Woolfs' first winter at Monks House was, according to Virginia, a decidedly medieval affair.

In the months before her death, with the noise of bombers droning overhead and the thud of distant gunfire, the blood red boxes that marched unchecked over the surrounding hills became associated in Virginia's mind with a much darker threat from across the channel. There was no escape; the only respite came at the end of each day as shadows lengthened and colour drained from the land:

Evening is kind to Sussex, for Sussex is no longer young, and she is grateful for the veil of evening as an elderly woman is glad when a shade is drawn over a lamp, and only the outline of her face remains. The outline of Sussex is still very fine. The cliffs stand out to sea, one behind another. All Eastbourne, all Bexhill, all St Leonards, their parades and their lodging houses, their bead shops and their sweet shops and their placards and their invalids and chars-`a-bancs, are all obliterated. What remains is what there was when William came over from France ten centuries ago: a line of cliffs running out to sea. Also the fields are redeemed. The freckle of red villas on the coast is washed over by a thin lucid lake of brown air, in which they and their redness are drowned.[89]

Chalk Paths, 1936, watercolour, Eric Ravilious

159

Throughout Virginia's last year, with the wail of sirens and the sound of anti-aircraft fire overhead, they lived each day in fear of a German invasion. Leonard was Jewish and the Woolfs, like many of their friends, had discussed the possibility of suicide if the enemy landed. This constant threat and the very real dangers posed by enemy bombs that shook the house almost certainly hastened Virginia's suicide. In her last note to Leonard she wrote: 'I feel certain I am going mad again.'[90] The south coast ports were badly hit; Virginia's diary recorded a direct hit on the Newhaven–Seaford train sustained on July 4th 1940 and from her favourite walk on the downs above Firle she could see the hospital ships returning from France. The skies above Rodmell were alive with dogfights during the Battle of Britain; a Messerschmitt was brought down on Caburn like 'a settled moth, wings extended'[91], and a Hurricane crashed at Southease, 'a little gnat, with red & white & blue bars'[92], provoking Virginia to complain 'so the Germans are nibbling at my afternoon walks.'[93]

The church and priory gatehouse, Wilmington

When bombs destined for the Alpha cement works breached the Ouse embankment in the autumn of 1940 the entire Ouse flats became one huge lake stretching from the garden of Monks House to the base of Mount Caburn and beyond. Virginia's walks along the valley were temporarily suspended and she rejoiced in the transformation; a landscape washed clean and made safe against the spreading rash of bungalows. The prospect from her studio beside the churchyard may also have brought to mind the equally disturbing vision – 'One sees a fin passing far out'[94] – that first surfaced in September 1926 as she neared the completion of *To The Lighthouse*. The image was only rendered safe by the completion of *The Waves* twelve years later: 'I have netted that fin in the waste of waters which appeared to me over the marshes out of my window at Rodmell ...'[95]

Sitting in the shadow of Rodmell church or up on Firle Beacon Virginia looked out to the ramparts of Mount Caburn's Romano-British camp and a more distant past. As far as the coast the bare chalk landscape is laced with prehistoric trackways, Celtic field systems and a succession of round barrows. In the opposite direction is a very different landscape. Arranged at the foot of the downs a mosaic of Saxon villages, Norman churches and Tudor mansions stretch away to the dark expanse of Ashdown Forest. Just beyond Charleston where Wilmington's chalk hill figure presides over the village with its churchyard yew, ancient and arthritic beside the priory gatehouse, these two landscapes converge dramatically.

Virginia's diaries are full of references to the wildlife of watermeadow and chalk grassland but there are few reminders of the ancient landscape through which she walked almost daily. Only in her last novel *Between The Acts* are the layers of history laid bare. Written in real time – events take place on a June afternoon in 1939 – this is ostensibly a novel about life in a country house and the village pageant in a community on the eve of war. Although Pointz Hall is deliberately placed well inland the novel draws heavily but obliquely on the author's sense of continuity and her years in Rodmell where the old families 'lay in their deaths intertwisted, like the ivy roots, beneath the churchyard wall.'[96] For Virginia the Sackvilles at Knole, the Sidneys at Penshurst (the Woolfs visited with Vita in June 1940) and the Leghs at Lyme Park in Cheshire (her review of 'The House of Lyme' appeared in the *TLS* in 1917) embodied this notion of the old order and, although conceived on a grander scale, these aristocratic outposts, too, are models for Pointz Hall. Virginia was also aware that while the history of the smaller manor house was often obscure – Teversal, Lawkland, Garsington and Kelmscott were among those she had known – they are equally important to our sense of the antiquity of England. But Pointz Hall, built in a hollow surrounded by wooded slopes

ENGLISH HOURS

and graced by a wide grass terrace, is a 'whitish house with the grey roof, and wing thrown out at right angles'[97] resembling the more immediate seat of feudal authority at Firle Place. Inside, the large, low-ceilinged bedrooms leading off a single corridor, recall the cool, beamed interior of Blo' Norton Hall in Norfolk (see Chapt. VII), 'a profound seat of solitude'[98] and, like Pointz Hall, 'near the very heart of England.'[99] But it is the great barn, lovingly evoked, in which teas are served during the pageant, that anchors the novel most firmly in the Sussex countryside.

The great barn, Alciston, 'a hollow hall, sun-shafted'

... as old as the church, and built of the same stone ... It was raised on cones of grey stone at the corners to protect it from rats and damp. ... The roof was weathered red-orange; and inside it was a hollow hall, sun-shafted, brown, smelling of corn ...[100]

The village pageant, depicting scenes from English history, was more like a medieval play than the Edwardian pageant of Empire and a popular form of entertainment between the wars. A more grand version of which Virginia would have been aware was E M Forster's 'England's Pleasant Land' performed on the lawn of his house in Surrey with music by Vaughan Williams. At Pointz Hall the money raised will go towards illuminating the parish church once the blackout is finally lifted but until then the floodlights dissecting the night sky serve a more sinister purpose. The pageant is a reminder of what people are fighting to preserve and is a form of escapism, a refusal to acknowledge the 'doom of sudden death'[101] hanging over the land. The swifts darting across in front of the barn like a squadron of enemy planes are part of the grand migratory cycle re-enacted each year since before the dawn of history while the nearly extinct Lucy Swithin, who reads H G Wells' *An Outline of History* each day, sits in contemplation of our descent from 'the iguanodon, the mammoth, and the mastodon.'[102]

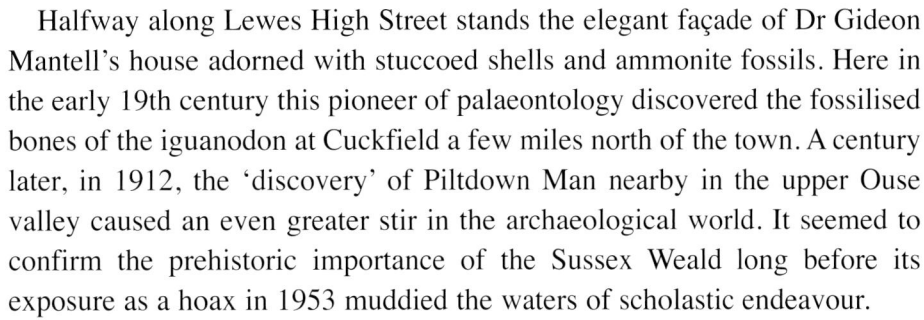

Halfway along Lewes High Street stands the elegant façade of Dr Gideon Mantell's house adorned with stuccoed shells and ammonite fossils. Here in the early 19th century this pioneer of palaeontology discovered the fossilised bones of the iguanodon at Cuckfield a few miles north of the town. A century later, in 1912, the 'discovery' of Piltdown Man nearby in the upper Ouse valley caused an even greater stir in the archaeological world. It seemed to confirm the prehistoric importance of the Sussex Weald long before its exposure as a hoax in 1953 muddied the waters of scholastic endeavour.

Although Virginia steadfastly refused all requests to write a play for the local Women's Institute she did reluctantly allow herself to become involved in rehearsals for the village play which bored her to distraction. Amateur dramatics were, she was convinced, devoid of imagination. She was more impressed by the imaginative power of rumour and used snatches of gossip and the polite rituals of daily life in *Between The Acts* to evoke a sense of community from which Miss La Trobe, driving force behind the pageant, feels increasingly isolated. The name, possibly from the architect Benjamin Latrobe who designed two late c18 houses in the Sussex Weald, marks her, like Virginia, as an outsider.

Ammonite motif, Mantell House

Gideon Mantell's house

Death by drowning was not uncommon in the Ouse. The bloated carcases of cattle, sheep and occasionally humans were from time to time dragged out of the river and the news of any disaster spread quickly along the valley. In August 1938 Virginia noted the death of an old woman 'who lived up at Mt Misery'[103] and whose body was recovered downstream near Piddinghoe, one of her own regular walks. Threatened with eviction this lonely individual 'used to moon over the downs with a dog'[104]. As she wrote those words the resemblance, at least outwardly, to her own predicament must have struck Virginia. She too was a familiar, often solitary, figure walking the marshes in her nightgown or muttering to herself up on the hills as her stories took shape.

On Christmas Eve 1940 the Woolfs lunched with Helen Anrep who had been Roger Fry's companion until his death in 1934. Anrep had rented a wing of Court House Farm, Alciston, an ancient pile incorporating part of the monastic grange to Battle Abbey. On a rise beside the church the medieval group, complete with enormous aisled tithe barn and ruined dovecote, is atmospheric still. Here, along the track from Charleston, Virginia felt a 'rush of love & envy'[105] for the place before recording one last ecstatic vision of her beloved Sussex:

> ... an incredible loveliness. The downs breaking their wave, yet one pale quarry; & all the barns & stacks either a broken pink, or a verdurous green; ... How England consoles & warms one, in these deep hollows, where the past stands almost stagnant.[106]

Alfriston, 1931 Shell poster, Vanessa Bell

Five months after the waters of the Ouse had receded Virginia was once more overwhelmed by 'this trough of despair.'[107] Despite her resolve she knew this time what she must do. In January 1941 she had called to mind a line from Walter de la Mare's 'Farewell':

> And I cant help even now turning to look at Asheham down, red, purple, dove blue grey, with the cross [of Rodmell Church] so melodramatically against it. What is the phrase I always remember – or forget. Look your last on all things lovely.[108]

ENGLISH HOURS

The Ouse at Southease

Stephen Tomlin's 1931 bust of Virginia in the garden at Monks House. Her ashes are buried nearby.

    She knew also that Asheham, covered in chalk dust and obliterated by the cement works, could never be reclaimed. Encircled by the same chalk hills that had sustained her for so long she set out one last time to walk across the meadows. Slipping into the cold, silt-laden waters of the Ouse the waves finally closed over her head.

SELECT BIBLIOGRAPHY

Barkway, Stephen, '"To Elevedon": Looking Over the Wall in Norfolk',
   Virginia Woolf Bulletin No.9, January 2002
   'Virginia In Yorkshire', Virginia Woolf Bulletin No.10, May 2002
Bell, Quentin, *Virginia Woolf, A Biography Vols. I & II*, Hogarth Press, 1972 & '73
Brown, Jane, *Spirits of Place*, Viking, 2001
Butts, M, *The Crystal Cabinet*, Beacon Press, 1988
Curtis, Vanessa, 'Talland House: Newly Discovered Material',
   Virginia Woolf Bulletin No.16, May 2004
   The Hidden Houses of Virginia Woolf and Vanessa Bell, Robert Hale Ltd, 2005
Dell, Marion, *Peering Through the Escallonia: Virginia Woolf, Talland House and St Ives* Bloomsbury Heritage Series 23, Cecil Woolf Publishers, 1999
   'Returning to St Ives: Virginia Woolf and Cornwall',
   Virginia Woolf Bulletin No.3, January 2000
   'Moments of Vision: Thomas Hardy and Virginia Woolf',
   Virginia Woolf Bulletin No.48, January 2015
   & Wybrow, Marion, *Virginia Woolf and Vanessa Bell: Remembering St Ives*,
   Tabb House, Padstow, 2003
Dunn, Jane, *A Very Close Conspiracy*, Pimlico, 1991
Forster, EM, *Howards End*, Penguin, 1989
   The Longest Journey, Penguin, 1989
Gayford, Martin, 'Still Winding and Wonderful: Zennor's Literary and Artistic
   Connections', Charleston Magazine No.19, Summer 1999
Hansen, Carol, *The Life and Death of Asham: Leonard and Virginia Woolf's
   Haunted House*, Bloomsbury Heritage Series 26, Cecil Woolf Publishers, 2000
Hardy, Thomas, *Tess of the d'Urbervilles*, Penguin, 1978
   Far from the Madding Crowd, Penguin, 1978
Harris, Alexandra, *Romantic Moderns*, Thames & Hudson, 2010
Hill-Miller, K, *From The Lighthouse To Monk's House*, Duckworth, 2001
Humm, Maggie, *Snapshots of Bloomsbury*, Tate Publishing, 2006
Hussey, Mark, *Virginia Woolf A-Z*, Oxford University Press, 1996
James, Henry, *English Hours*, Oxford University Press, 1981
Kilvert, Francis, *Kilvert's Diaries*, Penguin, 1977
Lee, Hermione, *Virginia Woolf*, Chatto and Windus, 1996
Lehmann, John, *Virginia Woolf*, Thames and Hudson, 1987
Lycett Green, Candida, *Betjeman's Britain*, Folio Society, 1999
Mitchell, WR, *Gossip from Giggleswick*, A Castleberg Publication (no date)
Mitchell, WS, *East Sussex: A Shell Guide*, Faber, 1978

Moore, Judy, *The Bloomsbury Trail in Sussex*, SB Publications, 1995
Morris, Jan (ed.), *Travels with Virginia Woolf*, Hogarth Press, 1993
Nicolson, Nigel, 'Virginia Woolf at Giggleswick', Transcript of Lecture given at Giggleswick School, April 1994
Noall, Cyril, *The Story of St Ives*, Tor Mark Press, 1994
Pevsner, Nikolaus, *West Yorkshire* (The Buildings of England), Penguin, 1959
    Wiltshire (The Buildings of England), Penguin, 1963
      & Newman, John, *Dorset* (The Buildings of England), Penguin, 1972
      & Nairn, Ian, *Sussex* (The Buildings of England), Penguin, 1965.
Pitt-Rivers, Michael, *Dorset: A Shell Guide*, Faber, 1966
Rudikoff, Sonya, *Ancestral Houses: Virginia Woolf and The Aristocracy*, Palo Alto, 1999
Spalding, Frances (ed.), *Paper Darts: The Illustrated Letters of Virginia Woolf*, Collins & Brown, 1991
Taplin, Kim, *The English Path*, The Boydell Press, 1979
Tolhurst, Peter, *East Anglia: A Literary Pilgrimage*, Black Dog Books, 1996
   Wessex: A Literary Pilgrimage, Black Dog Books, 1999
National Trust, *Virginia Woolf and Monks House*, National Trust, 1998
Warner, Sylvia Townsend, *Somerset*, Elek, P., 1949
Webb, Ruth, *Virginia Woolf*, (Writers' Lives), The British Library, 2000
Wright, Sarah Bird, *Staying at Monks House: Echoes of the Woolfs*, Bloomsbury Heritage Series 9, Cecil Woolf Publishers, 1995
Woolf, Virginia, *Jacob's Room*, Vintage, 1992
  To the Lighthouse, Penguin, 1992
  The Waves, Penguin, 1993
  Between The Acts, Penguin, 1992
  The London Scene: Six Essays on London Life, Random House, 1975
  Letters Vols. I-VI, Hogarth Press, ed. Nigel Nicolson and Joanne Trautmann, 1975-80
  Diaries Vols. 1-5, ed. Anne Olivier Bell, Penguin, 1979-85
  The Death of the Moth and Other Essays, Hogarth Press, 1942
  Essays Vols. I-IV, ed. Andrew McNeillie, Hogarth Press, 1986-88
      Vols. V & VI, ed. SN Clarke, Hogarth Press, 2009 & 2011
  The Complete Shorter Fiction, ed. Susan Dick, Hogarth Press, 1985
  A Passionate Apprentice: The Early Journals, ed. Mitchell A Leaska, Hogarth Press, 1990
  Moments of Being, ed. Jeanne Schulkind, Hogarth Press, 1985

NOTES

INTRODUCTION

1 *Travels with Virginia Woolf*, p.3
2 *Essays I*, p.124
3 *Essays II*, p.346
4 *A Passionate Apprentice (APA)*, p.285
5 *Letters I*, 282, p.234
6 *Essays I*, p.124
7 Ibid; p.124
8 *Essays II*, p.32
9 Ibid; p.163
10-11 *Essays I*, p.5
11A *Letters I*, 217, p.178
12 *Essays I*, p.32
13 *The London Scene*, p.31
14 *Essays I*, p.35
15-16 *Moments of Being (MOB)*, 2nd ed. p.128
17 *APA*, p.282
18 Ibid; p.149
19 *Letters I*, 26, p.27
20 *APA*, p.363-64
21 Ibid; p.364
22 Ibid; p.190
23 Ibid; p.194
24 Ibid; p.193
25 Ibid, p.205
26 Ibid; p.203
27 Ibid; p.301
28 *Letters I*, 266, p.221
29 *APA*, p.312
30-31 Ibid; p.310
32 *Letters I*, 282, p.234
33 Ibid; 427, p.341
34 Ibid; 380, p.307
35 *APA*, p.374
36 Ibid; p.372
37 *Complete Shorter Fiction*, p.117
38 *Diary I*, p.296
39 Ibid; p.278
40 Ibid; p.190
41 *Virginia Woolf*, Lee, H., p.434
42 Ibid; p.421
43 *Diary V*, p.357
44 *The Death of the Moth*, p.11
45 *Letters II*, 703, p.47
46 *Diary V*, p.346
47 *Travels with Virginia Woolf*, p.4

CORNWALL

1 *Life and Letters of Leslie Stephen*, p.345
2 *MOB*, 2nd ed. p.128
3 Ibid; p.131
4-5 Ibid; p.128
6 *MOB*, 1st ed. p.77
7 *MOB* 2nd ed. p.129-30
8 Ibid; p.131
9-10 Ibid; p.134
11 Ibid; p.133
12 Ibid; p.66
13 *Diary 2*, p.246
13A *MOB*, 2nd ed. p.65
14 Ibid, p.64-5
15-16 Ibid; p.66
17 Ibid; p.135
18-19 Ibid; p.71-2
20 *Jacob's Room*, p.47
21 *Hyde Park Gate News*, September 1892
22-23 *MOB*, 2nd ed. p.135
24 *Jacob's Room*. p.51
25 *Diary 2*, p.103
26 *Letters I*, 249, p.207
27 *APA*, p.282
28 Ibid; p.281-82
29 Ibid; p.282
30 *Letters I*, 249, p.207
31 *APA*, p.285
32 Ibid; p.286
33 Ibid; p.285
34 Ibid; p.289-90
35-36 Ibid; p.283
37-38 Ibid; p.292
39-40 Ibid; p.293
41-43 Ibid; p.294
44-45 Ibid; p.295
46 Ibid; p.297
47 Ibid; p.297-98
48 *Letters I*, 407, p.326

49   Ibid; 512, p.414
50   Ibid; 531, p.431
51-52 Ibid; 533, p.432
53   Ibid; 534, p.434
54-57 Quoted in 'Still Winding and Wonderful'
58   *Letters II*, 1069, p.379
59   *Diary 2*, p.105
60   *Letters II*, 1172, p.462
61   Ibid; p.460
62   Ibid; p.462
63   Ibid; 1255, p.532
64   Ibid; 1173, p.464
65   *Diary 3*, p.123
66   *Letters VI*, 3133, p.39-40
67   Ibid; 3134, p.40

THE BORDERS

1   *APA*, p.127
2   *Letters I*, 8, p.10
3   Ibid; p.9
4   Ibid; p.10
5   *MOB*, 2nd ed. p.102
6   *Letters I*, 8, p.10
7   *APA*, p.130
8   Ibid; p.132
9   *Letters II*, 709, p.51
10   *Letters VI*, 3404, p.242
11   Ibid; 3403, p.241
12   Ibid; 3408, p.246
13   *Diary 5*, p.150
14   Ibid; p.151
15-16 *Letters VI*, 3408, p.246

THE FENS

1   *Letters I*, p.25-6
2   *APA*, p.135
3-4 Ibid; p.136
5-6 Ibid; p.138
7   Ibid; p.138-39
8-9 Ibid; p.141
10   Ibid; p.142
11-12 Ibid; p.143
13   Ibid; p.140
14-15 Ibid; p.146
16   Ibid; p.148

17-19 Ibid; p.149
20   Ibid; p.144
21-23 Ibid; p.145
24   Ibid; p.149
25   Ibid; p.151
26   Ibid; p.156
27   Ibid; p.156-57
28   *Letters I*, 26, p.27
29-31 *APA*, p.161
32   *Virginia Woolf Vol. I*, Bell, Q, p.67

THE NEW FOREST

1-3 *APA*, p.202
4   Ibid; p.203
5   Ibid; p.216
6   *Letters I*, 203, p.168
7   Ibid; 206, p.172
8   *APA*, p.215
9-13 *Essays I*, p.53
14   *Letters I*, 330, p.270
15   *APA*, p.364
16   Ibid; p.363-64
17   Ibid; p.364

WILTSHIRE

1   *Letters I*, 98, p.91
2-3 Ibid; 99, p.92
4   *APA*, p.188
4A   *Wiltshire,* (The Buildings of England*)* p.317
5   *APA*, p.187
6-7 Ibid; p.192
8   Ibid; p.203
9   Ibid; p.190
10   Ibid; p.195
11   Ibid; p.196
12   Ibid; p.189
13   Ibid; p.198
14   Ibid; p.199
15   *Kilvert's Diary*, p.314
16   Ibid; p.314
17   *English Hours*, p.67
18   *APA*, p.199
19   Ibid; p.204
20   Ibid; p.205
21   Ibid; p.192

NOTES

22-23 Ibid; p.194
24   Ibid; p.193
25-26 Ibid; p.194
27   Ibid; p.193
28   *Letters II*, 711, p.52-3
29   *Letters IV*, 2174, p.163
30   *APA*, p.209
31   *Diary 2*, p.320
32-33 *Diary 4*, p.64
34-37 *Diary 4*, p.330

THE YORKSHIRE DALES

1   *Yorkshire: The West Riding*, p.217
2-5   *Letters I*, 193, p.156
6   Ibid; p.157
7   Ibid; 194, p.159
8   Ibid; 195, p.159-60
9-10 *Essays I*, p.6
11   Ibid; p.7
12   Ibid; p.5
13-15 Ibid; p.7
16-18 Ibid; p.8
19-20 *Letters I*, 266, p.221
21-22 *APA*, p.301
23   Ibid; p.302
24   Ibid; p.303
25   Ibid; p.304
26-27 Ibid; p.307
28   Ibid; p.302
29   Ibid; p.306
30-33 Ibid; p.305
34   *Diary 3*, p.142
35   Ibid; p.143
36   Ibid; p.144
37-39 *Diary 2*, p.101

EAST ANGLIA

1   *APA*, p.309
2   *Letters I*, 283, p.235
3   *APA*, p.310
4   Ibid; p.313
5   Ibid; p.312
6   Ibid; p.310
7   Ibid; p.312
8-9   Ibid; p.311

10   *Letters I*, 282, p.234
11-13 *APA*, p.311
14   *Letters I*, 282, p.234
15   *Complete Shorter Fiction*, p.47
16-24 *APA*, p.314
25   Ibid; p.316
26-29 Ibid; p.315
30-31 *The Waves*, p.11
32   *APA*, p.310
33   Ibid; p.315
34   Ibid; p.311
35   Ibid; p.310
36   Ibid; p.312
37   *Letters I*, 389, p.316
38   *Essays VI*, p.485
39   *Letters II*, 1075, p.384
40   Ibid; 746, p.83
41   Ibid; 775, p.107
42   Ibid; 776, p.108
43   Ibid; p.109
44-47 *Diary 4*, p.84
48-49 *Essays IV*, p.21
50   Ibid; p.20
51   Ibid; p.24
52-53 Ibid; p.20

RYE & ROMNEY MARSH

1   *Letters I*, 283, p.235
2-3   Ibid; 380, p.307
4   Ibid; 377, p.303-04
5   *APA*, p.372
6   Ibid; p.367
7   *Letters I*, 377, p.304
8   Ibid; 378, p.305
9   Ibid; 380, p.306
10   *APA*, p.367-68
11   Ibid; p.368
12-13 Ibid; p.369
14   Ibid; p.374
15-16 Ibid; p.372
17-18 Ibid; p.373
19-20 Ibid; p.371
21   Ibid; p.372
22   Ibid; p.371-72
23   Ibid; p.372
24-25 Ibid; p.374

171

SOMERSET

26	Ibid; p.369
27-28	Ibid; p.368
29	Ibid; p.369

SOMERSET

1	*Somerset*, p.7
2	*APA*, p.376
3	Ibid; p.376-77
4	*English Hours*, p.61
5	Ibid; p.62
6	Ibid; p.63
7	Ibid; p.64
8-9	*Letters I*, 426, p.340
10	Ibid; p.339
11	*APA*, p.378
12-13	Ibid; p.376
14-15	Ibid; p.378
16	Ibid; p.378-79
17-18	*Letters I*, 429, p.345
19	Ibid; 430, p.345
20	*APA*, p.379
21-22	*Letters I*, 431, p.347
23-24	Ibid; 435, p.352
25-26	Ibid; 437, p.354
27	Ibid; 427, p.341
28	*English Hours*, p.66
29-30	*Somerset*, p.20
31	*Letters I*, 426, p.340
32	*APA*, p.379
33	*Letters I*, 436, p.353
34	*Letters II*, 643, p.3-4

DORSET

1	*Howards End*, p.170
2	*Letters I*, 507, p.412
3	*Letters III*, 1432, p.76
3A	*Far from the Madding Crowd*, p.383
4	*Diary 2*, p.267
5	*Tess of the d'Urbervilles*, p.320
6-7	*Diary 2*, p.267
8-9	*Diary 3*, p.75
10	*Letters III*, 1630, p.256
11	*Dorset* (The Buildings of England), p.239
12	*Dorset: A Shell Guide*, p.124
13	*Diary 3*, p.75

14	*Letters III*, 1658, p.283
15	*Diary 3*, p.100
16	*Letters VI*, 3132, p.37
17	*Betjeman's Britain*, p.25
18-19	*Letters VI*, 3132, p.37

SUSSEX

1	*APA*, p.33
2	Ibid; p.34
3	Ibid; p.35
4	Ibid, p.71
5	Ibid; p.72
6	Ibid; p.74
7	Ibid; p.76
8	*Letters I*, 550, p.449
9	Ibid; 546, p.442
10	Ibid; p.443
11	Ibid, 561, p.456
12	Ibid, 566, p.462
13	Ibid; 567, p.462
14	Ibid, 571, p.467
15	Ibid, 582, p.476
16-17	Ibid; 563, p.458
18	*Diary 3*, p.156
19	*Beginning Again*, Woolf, L., p.48
20	Ibid; p.56
21	*Complete Shorter Fiction*, p.117
22	*Beginning Again*, p.57
23	*Letters I*, 602, p.489
24	*Beginning Again*, p.57
25	*Complete Shorter Fiction*, p.116
26	*Letters II*, 703, p.47
27	Ibid; 963, p.270
28-29	*Complete Shorter Fiction*, p.117
30-32	*Essays II*, p.40
33	*Diary 1*, p.48
34	*Letters II*, 954, p.263
35	Ibid; 876, p.185
36	Ibid; 918, p.227
37	Ibid; 695, p.42
38	Ibid; 674, p.31
39	Ibid; 790, p.120
40	Ibid; 746, p.83
41	*Diary 1*, p.151
42	Ibid; p.40
43	Ibid; p.45

NOTES

44	Ibid; p.41
45	Ibid; p.190
46-48	Ibid; p.278
49	Ibid; p.248
50	Ibid; p.249
51	Ibid; p.279
52-53	Ibid; p.286
54	Ibid; p.286-87
55-56	Ibid; p.286
57	Ibid; p.302
58-59	Ibid; p.296
60	*Diary 2*, p.4
61	Ibid; p.58-9
62	Ibid; p.155
63	*Diary 3*, p.138
64	*Diary 4*, p.109
65	*Diary 5*, p.72
66	*Diary 2*, p.62
67-68	Ibid; p.127
69	*Letters II*, 733, p.69
70	*Letters III*, 1516, p.146
71-73	*Diary 5*, p.357
74-75	*Diary 2*, p.134
75A	*The Crystal Cabinet*, p.16
76	*Letters II*, 1307, p.576
77	*Diary 4*, p.37
78	Ibid; p.62
79-80	*Complete Shorter Fiction*, p.143
81	*Diary 2*, p.70-71
82	*Diary 4*, p.124
83	*Diary 3*, p.159
84-85	*Complete Shorter Fiction*, p.229
86	*Diary 3*, p.154
87	*Diary 4*, p.85
88	*Diary 4*, p.124
89	*The Death of The Moth*, p.11
90	*Virginia Woolf, Vol II*, Bell, Q p.226
91	*Diary 5*, p.326
92-93	Ibid; p.300
94	*Diary 3*, p.113
95	*Diary 4*, p.10
96	*Between The Acts*, p.7
97	Ibid
98-99	*APA*, p.311
100	*Between The Acts*, p.18
101	Ibid; p.70
102	Ibid; p.8
103-4	*Diary 5*, p.161
105-6	Ibid; p.346
107	Ibid; p.354
108	Ibid; p.351

INDEX

Alciston **162**, 165
Aldeburgh **92**
Alfoxden House **115**, 116
Alfriston **165**
Allison, James 152
American Scene, The 101
Anrep, Helen 165
Arnold-Forster, Katherine ('Ka' Cox) 21, 22, 29, 92, 120, 126, 132
Arnold-Forster, Mark (Will) 21, 23, 24, 126
Arundel Castle 129, 131
Ashe of Rings 155
Austen, Jane 127, 128
Asheham (aka Asham) *x, xi, xii*, 18, 55, **135**-**36**, **137**-**38**, 139-40, 141, 143-44, 149, 158, 166
Avon, River (Wiltshire) 58

Barden Fell 78
Beckford, Peter 124
Bell, Clive *ix*, 17, 18, 49, 78, 97, 98, 101, 107, 110, 111, 114, 118, **119**, 155
Bell, Julian 118, 119
Bell, Quentin 43
Bell, Vanessa (see also Stephen, Vanessa) *i, ii, vi, ix*, 8, 17, 92, 93, **98**, 107, 118, 119, 123, 131, **136**, 140, **141**, 148, **155, 165**
Bemerton 51, **53**
Bennett, Alan 68
Benson, EF 102
Beresford, George **44**
Berlin, Sven **20**
Berryman's Farm 18
Betjeman, John 127
Between The Acts *ix, xi*, 161-63
Bindon Abbey **121, 122**
Bishop's Palace, Wells **112**
Blake, William 128
Blackmore, Vale of **122**, 123
Blo' Norton Hall *iii, iv, ix,* **79-83**, 89-90, 91, 97, 102, 162
Bloomsbury Group, The *ix,* 29, 93, 94, 117-120, 131, 136, 141, 148, 149, 158
Bognor Regis 128-**29**
Borders, The 25-31
Borrow, George *vi*

Boswell, James 58
Boudica, Queen 85
Bournemouth 117, 128, 154
Bowland Forest 75
Bradford-on-Avon 65
Bradshaw's Railway Guide 37
Bramptons, The 80
Breckland 87
Brighton 54, 128, **130**-31, **152**-53, 154
Broad Chalke 54
Brooke, Rupert 120
Brontës, The *vi*, 47, **71**
Brontë, Charlotte 71, 72
Brontë Society, The 72
Broomholm Priory **95**-96
Burton, Richard 152
Butts, Mary 22, 154-55

Caister Castle **95**, 96
Camber Castle **104**
Cambridge 1, 43, 67, 94
Carbis Bay 13, 14, 15
Carlyle, Thomas *vi*
Carrington, Dora **64, 65**, 94, 139
Case, Janet 21, 116, **141**
Castle Dinas 16
Cecil, Lady Robert 46, 98, 101, 115
Charles I 89
Charleston *ii, x,* 94, **140**, 141, 161, 165
Chaucer, Geoffrey 94, 95
Cheddar 112, 113
Chichester Harbour 48
Chilmark 45
Chollerford **29**, 30
Christchurch Priory 47, **48**, 49
Cilurnum 30
Cinque Ports, The 100
Clare, John *xi*
Coleridge, Samuel Taylor 115
Common Reader, The 125
Corby Castle 25, 26, **27**, 67
Corfe Castle 121
Cornhill Magazine, The 17, 126
Cornwall *i, ii, v, vii, viii, x,* 1-24, 29, 43, 49, 73, 91,

INDEX

118, 127, 131, 144
Cotswolds, The 25, 74
Crabbe, George 92
Cranborne Chase 123, 125
Cromwell, Oliver 37, 89
Cuckfield 163
Cuffnells 44

de la Mare, Walter 51, 165
Davies, Margaret Llewelyn 92
Denton 144
Devil's Dyke 130-31
Dew-Smith, Mrs 98
Dickens, Charles *vi*, 72
Dickinson, Violet *v*, 44, 47, 51, 67, 69, 70, 73, 92, 101, 108, 118, 125, 153
Diss *iii*
Dorset *ii, vii*, 22, 117-27, 131
Downlong 2, **3, 6,** 14
Dow, Thomas Millie 12
Draycott Terrace 16
Dryburgh Abbey 29
Duckworth, Gerald 8
Duckworth, Sarah ('Minna') 46
Duckworth, Stella 28, 128, 129
Duleep Singh, Maharajah 89
Duleep Singh, Prince Frederick 89-90

Eagle's Nest **21,** 22, 23
Earth Memories 143
East Anglia 79-96
Eastwood 67
Eden, Vale of **26**
Elveden Hall 87, **88,** 89
Ely 35
English Hours *i, iii, v,* 109
Eton 1

Fairford 66
Falmouth 24
Far from the Madding Crowd 126
Fastolf, Sir John 95
Feizor 76-**77**
Fens, The *ii, viii,* 32-**42, 43**
Firle *ix,* 18, 106, 131, 132, **142,** 144, 160
Firle Beacon **135,** 141, 161

Firle Place 131, **132,** 162
Fisher cousins 51, 130, 153
Fitzroy Square (No. 29) 106, 118, 131, 135
Forty Years On 68
Forster, E M 111, 117, 139-40, 163
Fritham House 44
Fry, Roger *xi,* 65, **118**-19, 132, 140, 165
Furze, Henry 51
Fyfield Down **62**

Gage family 131, 133
Gairdner, James 94
Garsington Manor 58, 139, 161
Gaskell, Elizabeth *vi,* **71,** 72
Garnett, Angelica **155**
Garnett, David ('Bunny') 92-3, 94, 140, 141
Gasthorpe **91**
Gawdy Bramptons, the, **82, 83**
Giggleswick 67-8, 72, 73, 74, 75, 77
Giggleswick School **68-9, 70,** 76
Gilsland 28, 30
Glastonbury Abbey *ix,* 46, 112, **113,** 114
Glastonbury Tor 108
Glazebrook family *xi,* **148**
Glyndebourne *xi*
Golden Bowl, The 101
Godmanchester 37, 38
Godrevy Lighthouse *vii,* **9,** 136
Gordon Square (No. 46) 67
Grant, Duncan 92-3, 94, **121,** 140, 141, 148
Gretna Green 28
Guardian, The *ii, vii,* 16, 47, 48, 70
Guthrie, Robin **62**
Gurnard's Head 8, **10,** 16, **18,** 22, 23

Haddon Hall 67
Hadrian's Wall 28, 29, 30, **31**
Halesworth 92, 93
Halsetown Bog 7
Ham Spray **64-5**
Hardwick Hall 67
Hardy, Thomas *ii, vi, vii,* 40, 121, 122, **125**
Harty, Russell 68
'Haunted House, A' 138
Haworth *vi, viii, ix,* 47, **71-2, 73,** 78
Hayle estuary 13, 17

175

Hazlitt, William xi
'Heard on the Downs: The Genesis of Myth' 138
Herbert, George 51, 53
Hill, Adrian **105**
Hills, Jack 25, 26, 27-8, 128, 129
Hills, Mrs 26, 27
Hogarth House 21
Hogarth Press *ii*, 23, 149, 155
Holford 116
Hopkins, Gerard Manley *x*
Hopton 82
Houghton **38**
Houghton Castle 30
Housesteads **30**-31
Hove **130**
Howards, Dukes of Norfolk 26, 28
Howards End 154
Hudson, W H 64
Huntingdon 32, 38, 41
Hyde Park Gate (No. 22) 3, 25, 32
Hyde Park Gate News 9

Iford 144, 149
Ingleborough 64
Inkpen Hill 81
Ismay, James 124
Itford Manor **144**
Iwerne Minster 123-**24**

Jacob's Room 8, 10
James, Henry *i, v, ix,* 5, 59, 79, 100, **101**, 102, 108-09, 114
Jefferies, Richard 55, 61, 83, 142
Jones, Inigo 56
Jonson, Ben 56
'Journal of Mistress Joan Martyn, The' *ix*, 83, 89
Jude the Obscure 123, 126

Keats, John *vi*
Kelmscott Manor **65**, 66, 161
Kelly's Directory 37
Kenninghall 83, **84**, 85, 86, 91
Kensington Gardens 3
Kent *iii*
Keynes, Maynard *vii*, 120-21, **155**
Kilvert, Francis 58-9

Knight, Dame Laura **24**
Knill's Monument **12**, 13
Knole *ii*, 58, 161

Lake District, The *vi*
Lamb, Henry 151
Lamb House 100-**01**
Lamb, Walter 132
Lands End 15
Lane End 46, 47, **49**
Lanercost Priory **28**
Lanyon Quoit **19**
Latrobe, Benjamin 163
Laughton Place **134**
Lawkland Hall **76**, 161
Lawrence, D H 18, 19-21, 23, 67
Lawrence, Frieda 19, 20
Lechlade 66
Lee, Hermione *x*, 138
Lelant **17**
Lelant Bay 13
Lewes *ix*, **131, 145**, 147, 158, **163-64**
Life and Letters of Leslie Stephen, The 49
Life of Charlotte Brontë, The *vi*, **71**, 72
Life of Delaine, The 17
Little Ouse River 100, 102, 108, 110, 114
Little Talland 132, **133**, 135
Lockeridge 62
London *ii, iii*
London Mercury, The 151
Longest Journey, The 111
Lopokova, Lydia **120,** 122
Lowell, James 5
Lulworth Cove 121
Lushington, Kitty 5
Lydgate, John 83
Lyttelton, Margaret 47
Lyme Park 161
Lyme Regis **126-27**
Lyrical Ballads *vii*, 115

MacCarthy, Desmond 132
MacCarthy, Molly 132, 139
Maitland, Frederick 49
Mansfield, Katherine 18, 19
Manorbier 115, 118

Manning Saunders, the 22
Mantell, Dr Gideon **163-64**
Market Weston Fen 91
Marlborough Downs 61-62
Marlowe, Christopher 56
Martin 64
Max Gate *ii*, *vii*, 125-26
Maxse, Leo 5
Mecklenburgh Square (No. 37) 158
Me, I'm Afraid of Virginia Woolf 68
Melymbrosia 133
Mendips, The 108, 111, 114, 115
Meredith, George 5
Millais, John Everett 43, 157
Milward, Blake 35-35
'Miss Pryme' 157
Moments of Being 7
Monks House *ii*, *x*, *xi*, 134, 144, **146-47, 149,** 150-52, **155-56**, 158, 159, 160, **167**
Morpeth, Lord and Lady 28
Morrell, Lady Ottoline 58, 110, 131, 137, 139
Morris, Jan *v*
Morris, William **65**, 66
Mortimer, Raymond 120
Mount Caburn *xi*, 146, **150, 151**, 161
Mrs Dalloway *iv*
Murry, John Middleton 19-20

Nadder Valley 51, 53-4
Nash, John **54**
Nash, Paul **102**
National Trust, The 102, 147, 154
Netherhampton House *viii*, 44, 51-**52**, 55, 60
Nether Stowey 115
Newbolt, Henry 51, 62
New Forest, The *viii*, 44-46, **47**, 48-50
Newhaven 154, 158
News from Nowhere **65**, 66
Nicolsons, the (Harold & Vita) 78
Night and Day *iv*, 93, 143
Norman, R C 58
North Tyne, River **29**-31
Northumberland 29-30

Old Sarum 58
Omega Workshop 148

Ouse, River (Sussex) *x*, *xii*, 135, 144, 146, 152, 163, 165, **166**
Outline of History, An 163

Painswick 25
Palgrave, Francis 127
Palmerston, Lord 44
Partridge, Ralph 64
Passionate Apprentice, A 16
Paston **96**
Pastons, The 94-96
'Pastons and Chaucer, The' 94
Paston Letters, The 83, 95
Peacehaven *xi*, **153**-54
Peak District, The 78
Peasmarsh 106
Pelhams, The 131, 134
Pembroke, Dowager Countess of 57
Pembroke, Earls of 52, 55, **56**, 57
Penshurst 161
Penzance 16, 17, 22
Persuasion 127
Pevsner, Nikolaus *iv*, 123, 147
Piercebridge 29
Playden **98**, 103
Poniou 22
Poole, Tom 115
Porthmear Beach 2
Porthminster Bay 11, 13, 14
Porthminster Hotel 9
Porthminster Point 15
Portraits of Places 59
Powys, Llewelyn 143
Powys, TF 117-18

Quantock Hills, The *vii*, **114**, 115, 116
Quidenham **85**-86

Radcliffe's Official Guide 53, 54
Rainbow, The 19
Ramsey 35, 36, 37, 43
Ramsey Abbey 35, **36**, 37
Rananim 19
Raverat, Gwen 98
Raverat, Jaques 120
Ravilious, Eric **103, 151, 158, 159**

Redgrave and Lopham Fen **91**
Richmond *ii*
Ringwood Manor 44
Roderick Hudson 59
Rodmell *iv, x, xi,* 55, 135, 144, 146-49, **150**, 151-52, 156-57, 160, 161
Romney Marsh *ix,* 97, 98
Romsey Abbey 44, **45, 46,** 47, 48
Rossetti, Dante Gabriel 66
Rother, River 99, 101
Round House, The **145**, 146, 147
Russell, Bertrand 22, 119
Rye *ii, ix,* **97,** 98, **99, 100,** 101-**03,** 104, 105
Rylands, George 120

Sackville-West, Vita *iii,* 24, 58, 134, 161
St Buryan **16**
St Erth 2, 3, 17
St Ives (Cornwall) *ii, v, vii, xii,* 1-2, **3-6,** 4-**12,** 13, **15,** 17, 18, 92
St Ives (Huntingdon) **37,** 38
Salisbury 51, 58,
Salisbury Cathedral *viii,* 44, 45, **60-61**
Sassoon, Siegfried 151
Scott, Sir Walter 29
Selborne, The Natural History and Antiquities of *x*
Sennen Cove 22, **24**
Sense of the Past, The 101
Settle 74
Seven Sisters, The **154**
Shaftesbury **123**
Shakespeare, William 56, 67
Shelley, Percy Byshe 66
Shepherd's Life, A 64
Sickert, Walter 2
'Sketch of the Past' *vii,* 7
Smyth, Dame Ethel 31, 62
Somerset *ii, vii,* 107-16
Somerset 114
Sorley, Charles 62
South Downs *x,* 102, **135, 138, 140,** 154, **159**
Southease 160, **166**
Southey, Robert 115
Spenser, Edmund 56
Stanhope, Lady Hestor 17
Steer, Philip Wilson 92

Stephen, Adrian 16, 35, 39, 49, 54, 97-**8,** 131, **138**
Stephen, Dorothea 32
Stephen, Julia *v,* 1, 5, 6-7, 9
Stephen, Leslie *vi-vii,* **1,** 5, 25, 44, 51, 67, 100, 126, 127, 129
Stephen, Thoby 8, 9, 26, 43, 44, 49, 82, 97,
Stephen, Vanessa **5,** 11, 14, 25, 27, 28, 39, 44, 49, 51, 53, 68, 79, 97, 102, 130
Stephen, Virginia (photographs of), **5, 44, 119, 141**
Steps, The **98**
Stiffkey Old Hall **94**
Stonehenge *viii,* 44, 58, **59,** 60
Strachey, Lytton 23, 43, 44, 62, **64,** 93, 101, 116, 118-19, 139
Strachey, Marjorie 136
Story of my Heart, The 142
Studland Bay 117, **118, 119**
Sussex *ii, vii, viii, ix, xi,* 3, 102, 128-66
Suto, Edward 117
Sydney-Turner, Saxon 18, 22, 43, 101, 140,
Sydneys, the 161

Talland House *ii, v, vii,* 1, **2,** 4, 7, 8-10, **11,** 12, 17, 44, 136
Tavistock Square (No. 52) *ii, iv,* 125, 158
Tees, River 29
Telscombe Down 142, **143,** 155
Tess of the d'Urbervilles 58, 121-22, 125
Teversal 67, 161
Thackeray, William Makepeace *vi,* 72
Thames, River 65-66
Thelnetham **90,** 91
Thetford *ix,* **86-87, 89,** 90
Thomas, Edward *vi, x,* **62**
Thomas, Jean 18
Thomson, James 29
'Three Pictures' 157
Tidmarsh Mill 64
Times, The 138
Times Literary Supplement *ii, vii,* 72, 126
Tintagel 18
Tomlin, Stephen **167**
To The Lighthouse *vii,* **8,** 37, 126, 161
Tregenna Castle 1, 5
Tregerthen 18, 22, 23
Tregerthen, Higher **21**

Trencrom 7, 13, 17
Treveal 11
Trevelyan, Bob 140
Trevose View 11
Twickenham 17

Vandyke, Sir Anthony 56, 57
Vaughan, Emma *viii*, 13, 32, 39, 43, 44, 51
Vaughan, Madge 69-71, 73
Vaughan, William 67, 68, **69**, 70
Vicars' Close, Wells **109**-10
Voyage Out, The 8, 107, 153
Voysey, Charles 117

Walberswick 92
'Walk by Night, A' *ix*, 16
Wallis, Alfred **14**
Warboys *viii*, **32-35**, 36, 41
Warboys Journal 39, 105
Warboys Rectory *viii*, 33, **36**, 37, 38-9, **40**, 52
Warner, Sylvia Townsend 107, 114
Warren, Edward **101**
Watling Street 29
Waves, The 8, 87-8, 89, 161
Webb, CC **31**
Wells 136-43
Wells Cathedral **107**, **108**-12, 115
Wells, HG 163
Wetherall Priory 27
Weymouth 127
Whistler 2
White, Gilbert *vi, x*
'Widow and the Parrot, The' 157
Wight, Isle of 44
Williams, Ralph Vaughan 163
Wilmington **160**, 161
Wilton *viii*, 52, **57**-8
Wilton House 44, 51, **55-6**, 57, 63-4
Winchelsea *ix*, 99, 103-**05**
Wissett Lodge 92, **93**
Wooler 29
Women in Love 19
Woodfords, The 58
Woodlanders, The 123
Woolbridge Manor **120**, **121**

Woolf, Leonard *i, vii, x*, 11, 24, 29, 62, 77, 78, 116, 144, 145-6, 149, 157, 160
Woolf, Virginia (photographs of), **155, 156, 166**
Wordsworth, Dorothy 115
Wordsworth, William *vi*, 44, 72, 115
Wordsworth's Cottage 29
Wyatt, TH 58
Wylye Valley 62

Years, The *iv*, 24
Yorkshire Dales, The *viii-ix*, 67-73, **74-5**, 76-8
Young, Hilton 107

Zennor 16, 18, 19, **20**, 22